Saints

The Art, the History,
the Inspiration

For
Nasseem
and in memory of
Katharine

Saints

The Art, the History,
the Inspiration

MICHAEL MCMAHON

How monotonously alike all the great tyrants and conquerors have been: how gloriously different are the saints.

C.S LEWIS

Introduction

Many people find it virtually impossible to think of the saints as real men and women. They do not see them as human beings with lively and complex personalities, but as sublimely elevated creatures—like statues that stand on plinths. Those statues often conform to a standardized version of holiness, so it's hard to imagine the saints they depict breaking into a laugh or a frown, or getting angry. And yet the more we learn about even the most dramatically holy of the saints, the more we realize how human they are.

In reality, their personalities are complicated and unique. St Teresa of Avila is widely known through Bernini's statue of her transported in ecstasy, a religious experience that she describes in her spiritual autobiography. Less well known are the human experiences that this same, vividly written story reveals. She had an observant eye and a keen understanding of character; in fact, she was not only a great saint, but a great writer. St. Hildegard of Bingen was also a nun, a writer and a mystic—and a fascinating personality of a very different sort. Her interests were quite unusually wide. She wrote commentaries on the creed, the Gospels and the Rule of St. Benedict—the sort of studies you might expect a saint to undertake—but she also wrote studies of medicine and natural history, and was a talented composer and artist. She set her religious lyrics to music, and drew intricate illustrations for her books.

Other saints led lives that were equally holy, but less colorful. St. Thérèse of Lisieux was a cloistered nun whose heroic inner struggles would have been unknown if her superiors had not ordered her to write her spiritual autobiography. There was nothing at all remarkable in the life of the Philipino layman St. Lorenzo Ruiz until he was accused of a crime, jumped on a boat to avoid capture, and found himself in Japan, where he was told that unless he renounced his Christianity, he would be tortured to death. He hesitated, for he was human; then he refused. "I did not come here to be a martyr," he said, "but because I could not remain in Manila. I now have to give up my life. Do with me what you wish." These are certainly not the words of a plaster saint.

Some find it hard to think of the saints as real people because so much that has been written about many of them is now beyond belief. When they read the claim that the infant St. Nicholas stood up and prayed for three hours during his first bath-time, they are tempted to throw out the saintly baby with his bath-water —which would be a mistake, for St. Nicholas certainly existed, even if that particular story about him was made up. St. George was a real character, too, though we know almost nothing about him for certain—except that he cannot possibly have slain his famous dragon. We now know that such creatures don't exist; but for people listening to the legend of St. George, dragons represented the devil incarnate—for them the devil *really* existed—and *that* was the point of having heroic saints such as George facing and overcoming dragons.

There was a time when such fanciful inventions made the saints seem powerfully real to those who heard or read them, but today, they can make them seem unbelievable and remote. We now know that some of the saints who have left the deepest mark on the common imagination have done so not through their lives, but through their

previous page 2: **St. Basil, 18th century, Croatian**
St. Basil is Dubrovnik's protector and patron saint.
previous page 4: **Saint Mark, Guariento di Arpo, c. 1338–78, Italian**

legends. This does not mean that we should discount their lives or dismiss the stories, but it does mean that we can only guess what they may have been like as real people. Sometimes, those legends can offer clues, for the kind of stories that were told of saints can suggest the kind of virtues they possessed. The few facts that we know about St. Brigid are vastly outnumbered by unhistorical anecdotes about her miracles, tales of turning water into beer to cater for unexpected guests, or of multiplying pats of butter to feed the poor, and similar examples of generous compassion. They may not be literally true, but the pattern of them at least suggests something of the character of the saint that inspired them.

Encountering modern saints as real people is much easier, for there are no legends to get in the way. We can see exactly what they looked like from their photographs. We can watch television footage of Mother Teresa of Calcutta, who was beatified in 2003. We can see for ourselves the love that she gave, and the love her sisters still give, to the dying and the destitute. We can visit the cell in Auschwitz where St. Maximilian Kolbe was murdered in 1941. We know enough about the wicked reality of that and places like it to appreciate the courage and generosity of the man who volunteered to die there so that another might live.

Modern saints like these remind us that despite differences of circumstance and personality, the saints of all ages have one thing in common: a love of God that is absolute, and which shapes everything they say, think, and do. The more we get to know them, the more we realize that this love does not extinguish their individuality, but enhances it. The saints are uniquely special, and equally approachable: we are invited to admire them for their saintliness, and to look upon those whose examples touch us particularly as our friends.

In the saints, one thing becomes clear: those who draw near to God do not withdraw from men, but rather become truly close to them.

BENEDICT XVI, *GOD IS LOVE,* 2006

following page: **St. Francis Receives the Stigmata, Domenico Ghirlandaio, 1449–94, Italian**
Christ appears to Francis with wings of a seraphim, and marks the saint's body with the stigmata.

chapter 1
Saints and Sainthood

What is a Saint?

It is not those that commit the least faults who are most holy, but those who have the greatest courage, the greatest generosity, the greatest love.

ST. FRANCIS DE SALES

All religions identify people who are outstanding for their holiness; Christianity calls its holy men and women "saints." The term was originally used to describe *all* Christians. For instance, St. Paul addressed the Christian community of Ephesus as "the saints who are also faithful in Christ Jesus" (Ephesians 1: 1); and St. Peter visited "the saints who lived at Lydda" (Acts 9: 32). Later, the term ceased being used for the living, and referred only to the dead—people who had been so particularly holy in this life that their place in Paradise was beyond doubt.

The first Christians to be recognized as saints in this latter sense were those who were put to death for their faith. They were called "martyrs," a Greek word that means "witness": a martyr witnesses to his faith by dying for it. The first Christian martyr was St. Stephen, who was stoned to death in about the year 35. His executioners were fellow-Jews, but most early martyrs were put to death by Romans, who saw the followers of Jesus of Nazareth as a threat to the stability of the state.

right: The Lapidation of St. Stephen, Jean Fouquet, reproduced in *Oeuvre de Jehan Foucquet*, 1866–7, French
St. Stephen, the first Christian martyr is shown being stoned to death.

Until the beginning of the fourth century, there were frequent persecutions in which many Christians were martyred—but against all human odds, the new religion not only survived, it flourished. Christian communities sprang up in every corner of the Roman empire, inspired by the heroism of the martyrs and the preaching of Christ's disciples, most particularly that of St Paul, whose three great missionary journeys to Cyprus, to Asia Minor, eastern Greece, and Ephesus helped spread the faith among the Gentiles.

By the time that the persecutions and the martyrdoms ended, Christians had begun to recognize other types of holy heroes, whom they called "confessors." Among the first of them were ascetics such as St. Antony of Egypt (251–356) and renowned warriors for orthodoxy such as the patriarch of Alexandria, St. Athanasius (296–373).

Soon, the description "saint" came to be used for martyrs and confessors rather than for the more ordinary members of the church. The earliest saints were not granted their titles formally—they won them by popular acclaim. From about the sixth century onward, local bishops began to reserve the right to decide whether or not someone had been a saint. They would make inquiries about that person's life and teachings to make sure that only those who had been holy to a heroic degree could be "canonized"— that is, added to the official list (or canon) of saints. It later became customary to pass these decisions to Rome for papal approval and in the thirteenth century, Rome ruled that all future canonizations had to be formally authorized by the pope.

Since then, several popes have reformed and revised the procedures by which individuals are declared to be saints. The most recent revision was carried out by Pope John Paul II in 1983. The current rules dictate that a candidate's cause (the formal process by which a person's sainthood is verified) cannot proceed until five years after he or she has died—though this restriction can be waived, as it was in the case of John Paul himself, whose cause was opened only eighty-seven days after his death.

Evidence is gathered locally at first, and the case is then passed to the Vatican's Congregation for the Causes of Saints. If after an examination of the subject's life, deeds, and writings, the Pope accepts that he or she has practiced the Christian virtues to a heroic degree, he awards him or her the title "Venerable." The next step on the stairway to sainthood is beatification, which is the award of the Latin title *Beatus* which means "Blessed." To achieve this, it must be shown that prayers to the candidate resulted in a miracle, such as a medical cure for which there is no scientific explanation. A *Beatus* is given a feast day that is observed in a particular region or by a religious order. A second miracle is required before a *Beatus* can formally be declared a saint, and universally venerated. The procedure is slightly different for martyrs, who do not need a miracle for beatification.

The saint is a medicine because he is an antidote. Indeed that is why the saint is often a martyr; he is mistaken for a poison because he is an antidote. He will generally be found restoring the world to sanity by exaggerating whatever the world neglects, which is by no means always the same element in every age. Yet each generation seeks its saint by instinct; and he is not what the people want, but rather what the people need.

G.K. CHESTERTON

And suddenly there came a sound from heaven as of a rushing mighty wind, and it filled all the house where they were sitting. And there appeared unto them cloven tongues like as of fire, and it sat upon each of them. And they were all filled with the Holy Ghost, and began to speak with other tongues, as the Spirit gave them utterance.

ACTS 2: 3,4

left: **Pentecost, fresco, artist unknown, Saint Sebastien Chapel, Lanslevillard, c. 1446, French**
Fifty days after his resurrection, Jesus' followers were dramatically endowed with the miraculous power to speak in any language and be understood. By this gift they were able to spread the message of Christianity throughout the different countries and cultures of the Roman Empire.

Saints as Intercessors

Oh, that one might plead for a man with God, as a man pleadeth for his neighbor!

JOB 16:21

The need for intercession is poignant, and it is the saints who can be successfully invoked to plead the case of erring humans. They are not only looked to as examples, but also for moral and spiritual support. Christians have prayed to saints to petition God on their behalf since the earliest days of the church. In the third century, St. Cyprian (200–258), bishop of Carthage, wrote of the power of the martyrs to intercede for others after death (he was himself martyred in 258.) St. Cyril of Jerusalem (315–387) and St. John Chrysostom (347–407) also wrote to similar effect. Named saints were honored in the principal act of Christian worship, the Eucharist. They still are. But it is not only the great or famous saints that are called upon by the faithful—as St. Thomas Aquinas pointed out in his *Summa Theologia* "it is sometimes profitable to pray to the lesser [saints] ... because sometimes one has greater devotion for a lesser saint than for a greater, and the effect of prayer depends very much on one's devotion."

right: **St. John Chrysostom, *Butler's Lives of the Saints,* 18th century**
The popular archbishop of Constantinople strongly advocated praying to saints to intercede with God.

God … stirs up in human beings a love of virtue; and he inspires some to become saints, in order to be an example to the others.

ST. BASIL

The saints on earth and those above
But one communion make;
Joined to their Lord in bonds of love,
All of His grace partake.

ISAAC WATTS

… saints will aid if men will call;
For the blue sky bends over all!

SAMUEL TAYLOR COLERIDGE

Christ lives in his saints.
We know his life in them.

EDWARD KING, BISHOP OF LINCOLN

And men see his good works, and admire
them in spite of themselves, and see that they
are Godlike, and that God's grace is no dream,
but that the Holy Spirit is still among men, and
that all nobleness and manliness is His gift,
His stamp, His picture: and so they get a
glimpse of God again in His saints and heroes,
and glorify their Father who is in heaven.

CHARLES KINGSLEY

A man does not have to be an angel in order to be a saint.

ALBERT SCHWEITZER

What makes saintliness in my view, as
distinguished from ordinary goodness, is a
certain quality of magnanimity and
greatness of soul that brings life within the
circle of the heroic.

HARRIET BEECHER STOWE

Patron Saints

I have three patron saints: I need three patron saints to keep me out of trouble. The one is St Francis of Assisi, the other is Theresa, the Little Flower. I was attracted to her in the hope that she would help me to learn to be small. And then I have had a particular fondness for Mary Magdalene. But I have become, as you probably have become, more and more aware of just how contemporary St Francis and his concerns have come to be.

ARCHBISHOP DESMOND TUTU, JERUSALEM, DECEMBER 23RD, 1989

From the eighth century onward, biographies of the saints were read during the divine office, the daily routine of prayer undertaken by monks, priests, and nuns. This did much to spread knowledge of saints' lives—not all of it accurate—and led to individual saints being associated with particular causes, places, or professions, of whose interests they were seen as heavenly protectors. The tradition that St. Luke had been a painter made him the obvious patron saint of artists. The story that St. Sebastian had been shot with arrows led to his patronage of archers. The Life of the apostle St. Bartholomew describes how he was flayed alive during his martyrdom: he became patron of all those who work with skins, including tanners and glovemakers. The fictional life of the real St. Dorothy (d. c. 304) describes how a young man mocked her on her way to her martyrdom by asking her to send him some flowers from paradise when she got there; an angel appeared and gave him a basket of apples and roses. St. Dorothy is thus the patron of flower-sellers.

Modern occupations have patron saints, too, some of them chosen with wit. St. Joseph of Copertino (1603–63), who was famous for his frequent levitations, is the patron saint of astronauts.

Plague-sufferers prayed to St. Roch (1350–80), who had himself suffered from that disease. The mistaken belief that St. Erasmus had been martyred by having his entrails pulled out led to those afflicted by stomach ailments to call upon his help. The legendary life of St. Blaise, which records him as martyred in the early fourth century, includes an incident in which his prayers saved a child choking on a fish bone. He was therefore invoked by people with sore throats. The unhistorical legend of the real St. Vitus (d. c. 303) claims that he cured the epileptic son of the emperor Diocletian. His help was thus sought by sufferers from epilepsy and from the eponymous disease, St. Vitus' Dance.

Popular opinion in towns, cities, and countries put those places under the patronage of particular saints. Sometimes this was because the saints were born there, worked there, or evangelized them; sometimes, because they were the resting place of their relics. The fame of St. Francis (1181–1226) made him the obvious patron of Assisi (and, later, with St. Catherine of Siena, of Italy.) St. Martin of Tours (c.316–97) is another saint defined by his relationship with a town. The monk who had been a Roman soldier was its bishop.

Germany's patrons are St. Boniface (675–754) and St. Anskar (801–65), the monk from Amiens who became archbishop of Bremen. Spain is one of many countries under the protection of the Blessed Virgin Mary: she is joint patron with St. James the Greater, whose relics are claimed by the pilgrim city of Compostela. Most people know that St. Patrick is patron saint of Ireland but it is less well known that London's patron saint is its seventh-century bishop, St. Erkenwald.

I am Patrick, yes a sinner and indeed untaught; yet I am established here in Ireland where I profess myself bishop. I am certain in my heart that "all that I am," I have received from God. So I live among barbarous tribes, a stranger and exile for the love of God ...

ST. PATRICK

right: **Saint Patrick Journeys to Tara, Vittorio Bianchini, 20th century, Italian**
Patrick had an eventful life—he was kidnapped as a child and shipped to Ireland. He escaped from there to Europe, and years later was sent back to convert the Irish, making the country a stronghold of Christianity.

I bear a basket lined with grass;
I am so light, I am so fair,
That men must wonder as I pass
And at the basket that I bear,
Where in a newly-drawn green litter
Sweet flowers I carry—sweets for bitter.

GERARD MANLEY HOPKINS, *FOR A PICTURE OF ST. DOROTHEA*

right: **Dorothea and the Roses, Henry Ryland, c. 1880–1924, English**
The saint is the special patron of flower sellers.

... people came daily to him for to recover their health in so much that the holy man saw that of needs he must make his habitation or housing more spacious and greater than it was, and thought to him good and necessary to make a great garden, wherein he should have all manner of herbs good for to make pottage with, for to feed the poor when they should return towards him, and so he did.

THE GOLDEN LEGEND: *THE LIFE OF SAINT FIACRE*

left: **15th-century French painting of St. Fiacre in his garden, reproduced in *Les Arts Somptuaires*, 1857–8, French**
This patron saint of gardeners was a 7th-century Irish hermit who settled in France.

Archangel-saints

Revelation describes seven archangels who stand before the Throne of God, and three of them are given names: Gabriel, Michael, and Raphael. These three are regarded as saints. All angels are messengers—the word *angelos* means "messenger" in Greek—and Gabriel's key role in the Annunciation makes him the bearer of the most important message of all time. Gabriel's name means "the mighty one of God." In the Old Testament, he helps Daniel interpret his visions; in the New Testament, he informs Zachariah that he will become the father of St. John the Baptist; and he tells the Virgin Mary that she will give birth to Jesus. He is therefore the obvious choice as patron saint for those who work in the field of communications. That patronage includes telephone and postal workers, radio operators, couriers, journalists and all those who work in telecommunications and the mass media.

The angel Gabriel from heaven came,
His wings as drifted snow, his eyes as flame.

BASQUE CAROL, TRANS. SABINE BARING-GOULD

right: **Annunciation, Orazio Gentileschi, 1563–1639, Italian**
Gabriel, the powerful archangel and saint is also honored in Islamic tradition, where he is regarded as chief of the four favored angels, and the spirit of truth.

St. Raphael

Raphael, whose name means "God heals," appears in the Old Testament in the apocryphal Book of Enoch and in the Book of Tobit. In the former, he heals the earth after it has been defiled by the fallen angels. In the latter, he heals Tobit's blindness; the story says that Tobit sends his son Tobias on a journey, and the boy is accompanied by the Archangel in disguise. Raphael helps him to catch a fish, which is then used to cure Tobit's blindness. A fish is usually found in depictions of him.

Tradition also identifies him as the angel who moved the waters of the pool described in St. John (5: 1–4), where Jesus healed the crippled man on the Sabbath.

right: Tobias and the Angel, Adam Elsheimer, 1578–1610, German
Raphael's help for Tobias on his journey has established him as one of the patron saints of travelers.

St. Michael

St. Michael (whose name means "Who is like God?") appears in the Old Testament in the Book of Daniel and in the New Testament in Revelations and the Epistle of St. Jude. He leads the heavenly host in battle against the devil, and is easily recognized in art by his sword and a conquered dragon—although he is sometimes shown in his other role, weighing souls at the Day of Judgment. His influence has always been considered very powerful, and devotion to him as a protector against the forces of evil is ancient. Constantine the Great (288–337) dedicated a church to him near Constantinople.

His cult was strengthened by his apparition on Mt Gargano toward the end of the fifth century. Other visions led to the foundation of St. Michael's Mount in Cornwall in the eighth century, and of Mont-Saint-Michel in France in the tenth. St. Michael is the patron saint of warriors in general and paratroopers in particular, of police officers, swordsmen, and manufacturers of scales and balances.

The three archangels are now commemorated together on Michaelmas Day, September 29th, which is renamed the feast of St. Michael and All Angels.

left: **The Archangel Saint Michael, 20th century, Peruvian School**
During the 17th century Peruvian artists were trained by the Spanish to produce paintings in the style of Spanish and Flemish masterpieces. This tradition exists to the present day in the city of Cuzco, Peru.

The Calendar of Saints

Saints have been remembered on particular days since earliest Christianity. In Christian countries, before literacy became widespread, most people did not identify dates by months and numbers, but by reference to saints' days or church feasts. When Shakespeare's Henry V makes his great speech before the battle of Agincourt, he does not tell his troops that their heroism will be remembered every October 25th, but every time the feast of SS. Crispin and Crispinianus comes round:

This day is called the feast of Crispian:
He that outlives this day, and comes safe home,
Will stand a tip-toe when this day is named,
And rouse him at the name of Crispian.

The days on which the early martyrs died were regarded as their heavenly birthdays, and the anniversaries of their deaths were marked by the celebration of the Eucharist at their tombs. Christian communities compiled registers of these dates, called martyrologies. As saints who had not been martyred began to be recognized, their names were included, too. These local lists were shared with other churches and then combined into comprehensive calendars such as the fifth-century Hieronymian Martyrology named after the Latin form of St. Jerome (341–420), who was wrongly believed to be its author. Later historical martyrologies included those compiled by St. Bede (673–735), and the ninth-century Benedictine monks, SS. Ado and Usuard. These form the basis of the definitive Roman Martyrology, first published in 1584 and revised many times since, most recently in 2004. This, in turn, forms the basis of the calendar of saints.

With so many thousands of saints commemorated, it is simply not possible to celebrate them all individually in a year, and the church remembers only the more famous of them on each day. Many saints' days that are not universally observed are celebrated by local churches and religious orders. The rest are honored on All Saints' Day, November 1st. In the Catholic world, work stopped on major saints' days and church feasts such as Christmas, Easter, and Corpus Christi (which commemorates the gift of Christ's presence in the Eucharist).

Everyone was obliged to attend mass. Some saints' days were observed in this way everywhere; others were celebrated locally. Even today, countries with a secular constitution but a Catholic inheritance (such as France) keep the feast of the Assumption of the Blessed Virgin Mary (August 15th) as a public holiday. In 1969 the Roman calendar was revised by the Vatican. Modern scholarship had shown that some of the saints whose feast days were celebrated had never existed; legendary saints such as St. Barbara and St. Margaret of Antioch had been included by mistake. Their feasts were dropped.

Many very real saints such as the Martyrs of Uganda, Korea, and Australasia who had hitherto been venerated only on their home ground, were now included in the universal calendar, emphasizing the international nature of the church. Some saints' days were moved back to dates from which they had been displaced, and others were transferred so that they would not fall in the penitential seasons of Advent or Lent. The most significant change to the calendar since 1969 has been its enlargement— 482 saints were canonized by Pope John Paul II, more than had been created during the previous four centuries. The list ranges from the twelfth-century bishop of Riga, St. Meinardo, to the twentieth-century Spanish priest, St. Josemaría Escriva de Balaguer (1902–75), founder of Opus Dei.

Tis the years midnight, and it is the dayes,
Lucies, who scarce seaven houres herself unmaskes,
The Sunne is spent, and now his flasks
Send forth light squibs, no constant rayes;
                                          The worlds whole sap is sunke

JOHN DONNE, *A NOCTURNALL UPON ST. LUCIES DAY, BEING THE SHORTEST DAY*

right: **St Lucia, David Ljingdahl,** *Allers Familj-Journal,* **1927, Swedish**
Saint Lucy's day (December 13th) In Sweden, the girl chosen to be Lucia
carries coffee and cakes to those preparing Christmas gifts and decorations.

Saint Catherine's Day

NOVEMBER 25TH

Sweet St Catherine,
A husband, St Catherine,
Handsome, St Catherine,
Rich, St Catherine,
Soon, St Catherine!

TRADITIONAL SONG FOR ST. CATHERINE'S DAY

left: **St Catherine Fête, *Le Petit Journal,* 1913, French**
St. Catherine is the patron of single women, and her feast-day, November
25th is a traditional holiday for Paris shopgirls. Here, a procession of cheerful
"Catherinettes" parade along the Rue de la Paix, dressed in elaborate hats.

Saint Swithin's Day

St. Swithin's day if thou dost rain
For forty days it will remain
St. Swithin's day if thou be fair
For forty days 'twill rain nae mair.

FOLK SAYING

right: **St. Swithin's Day, Robert Dudley, *Monthly Maxims*, c. 1887, English**
According to tradition, if it rains on July 15th (St. Swithin's Day) it will continue to rain for the following 40 days. St Swithin (d. 862) was bishop of Winchester. When his remains were reinterred in 971, there was a spectacular rainstorm.

Saint Valentine's Day

FEBRUARY 14TH

Hail, Bishop Valentine, whose day this is,
   All the Aire is thy Diocis
   And all the chirping Choristers
And other birds are thy Parishioners,
   Thou marryest every yeare.

JOHN DONNE: *ON THE LADY ELIZABETH AND COUNT PALATINE*
BEING MARRIED ON ST. VALENTINE'S DAY

left: **St. Valentine, Eleanor Fortescue Brickdale,** *Old English*
Songs & Ballads, **c. 1918, English**
Depicted here as a boy bishop, Valentine is commemorated on February
14th, the day when birds are supposed to mate. Over the centuries, his
patronage inevitably became transferred to the arena of human courtship.

Fra Angelico

Fra Angelico—"the Angelic Friar"—is the name by which the English-speaking world knows the Tuscan painter Guido di Pietro (1387–1455), one of the most gifted artists of the Quattrocento. He adopted the religious name "Giovanni" when he became a Dominican monk (in continental Europe, he is more accurately called Beato Angelico.) A man who was both gifted and holy, Fra Giovanni of Fiesole has a place not only in Vasari's *Lives of the Artists,* but also in the calendar of saints.

He was a Renaissance artist who painted only religious subjects, creating works that convey a mystical tenderness and serenity. For Fra Angelico, as for the icon-painters of the Orthodox tradition, painting was an act of prayer. His status as a *beatus* is also special, because he won it by popular acclaim shortly after his death, long after the church had introduced rules requiring a formal process for beatification.

His reputation for piety—and his paintings, which are a reminder of it—made it unthinkable that his title as "Blessed Angelico" should be challenged. However, it was not formally recognized until 1983, when Pope John Paul II declared him to be "equivalently beatified." When the subject of the necessary miracle was brought up, the pope pointed to Fra Angelico's frescoes in the Vatican and said, "These are his miracles." The following year, he proclaimed Fra Angelico patron saint of artists.

right: **St. Lawrence, fresco, Fra Angelico,1387–1455, Italian**
St Lawrence is shown distributing alms. The Chapel of St. Nicholas in the Vatican at Rome contains luminous frescoes by Fra Angelico depicting the Lives of St. Lawrence and St. Stephen, The Four Evangelists, and The Doctors of the Church.

Decoding the Pictures

Christian art has always used symbols. Some of the most ancient are found in the catacombs, the network of underground tunnels in which the early Roman Christians buried their dead. The image of a dove was used to represent the Holy Spirit; a fish or a shepherd represented Christ; a ship symbolized the church; an anchor, salvation; a peacock, immortality. These simple images used by the earliest Christians did not attract the attention of their persecutors, for they were commonly used in non-Christian art, also.

When the persecutions stopped and Christians could conduct themselves openly, they adorned their places of worship with explicit images of Christ and the Apostles and saints. Sometimes, those pictures were labeled, but few people were able to read, so the characters who were depicted were identified by special symbols that were associated with them. Over the centuries, a kind of visual language developed, and the emblems (or combinations of emblems) that identify individual saints became fixed.

right: **Christian wall paintings, Calixtus Catacombs, Rome, Illustrations after G.B de Rossi *Roma Sotterranea Christiania*, 19th-century, Italian**
The catacombs (underground cemeteries) where early Christians were buried are decorated with pictures rich in Christian imagery.

SCS
PE
TR
VS

☩ SCISSIMVS

DN
LEO
PP

☩ DN CARVLO

REGI

Saints and their Emblems

An image of a man holding keys would be recognized instantly as St. Peter, to whom Christ had given the keys of the Kingdom of Heaven (Matthew 16: 19). The four Evangelists are all shown with a book, representing their gospels, plus a second emblem that identifies them individually. The origins of these are the four winged creatures described in the vision of St. John himself in the Book of Revelation. St. Matthew's emblem is a winged man. Another of his identifying signs is the halberd, sword, or spear. Occasionally, there is a moneybag in the picture, signifying his earlier calling as a tax collector.

St. Mark's emblem is a lion, perhaps because his gospel begins with the story of St. John the Baptist preaching in the wilderness, where lions live. St. Luke is identified by a sacrificial ox, because his gospel begins with the sacrifice made by St. John the Baptist's father, Zachariah. St. John's own symbol is an eagle; he is also sometimes depicted with a chalice and a serpent. A legend tells how, after he was made to drink poison for refusing to sacrifice to pagan gods, he blessed the cup and the evil in it fled in the form of a poisonous snake.

And I say also unto thee, That thou art Peter, and upon this rock I will build my church; and the gates of hell shall not prevail against it.
And I will give unto thee the keys of the kingdom of heaven.

MATTHEW 16: 18, 19

left: **Mosaic, 9th century, Italian**
St. Peter is traditionally depicted with the keys bestowed upon him by Jesus.

Saints and their Garments

It is very easy to identify St. Paul in any artistic depiction—he is always shown with a combination of emblems—a book (his epistles) and the sword with which he was executed. But depending on the century in which he was depicted, his style of garments varies.

Clothing is a good way of identifying ecclesiastical rank, but it invariably represents the age in which the art is created. The first-century martyr St. Stephen is always shown wearing a dalmatic, a particular vestment worn by deacons. St. Jerome (c. 340–420) is usually depicted wearing the broad-brimmed red hat of a medieval cardinal, because he had briefly been a papal secretary. A cardinal's hat is also an identifier of St. Robert Bellarmine (1542–1621), the Jesuit prelate who lived on bread and garlic, and had the curtains of his official apartments given to clothe the poor.

And we know that to them that love God all things work together unto good: to such as, according to his purpose, are called to be saints.

ST. PAUL'S EPISTLE TO THE ROMANS: 8: 28

left: **St. Paul, Peter Paul Rubens, 1577–1640, Flemish**
The saint holds the two iconic objects (the sword and his book) that immediately identify him as Paul to the viewer.

Other Saintly Signs

Some saint's symbols are derived from puns on their names. The emblem of St. Agnes (d. 305) is a lamb, because of the similarity of her name to the Latin word, *agnus*. The third-century pope and martyr St. Cornelius is shown holding a horn, for which the Latin is *cornus*. The link between the Latin word for light, *lux,* and the name of St. Lucy (d. 304) is probably the starting point for the legend that she had her eyes pulled out prior to her martyrdom. Her emblem is a pair of eyes.

Other tortures, real or invented, give rise to some fairly gruesome symbols. The emblem of St. Agatha is her breasts, which are cut off in her unhistorical legend. They are sometimes shown carried on a dish. St. Catherine (whose legend claims that she was martyred in the fourth century) is shown with her wheel. St. Lawrence (d. 258) is invariably shown with the gridiron on which he was said to have been roasted to death. The third-century martyr St. Denys (or Dionysius) carries his own severed head. The emblem of Pope St. Clement, martyred at the end of the first century, is an anchor. His unreliable life story describes how he was thrown into the sea with an anchor tied round his neck.

Pictures and statues with such emblems were well understood: Pope St. Gregory the Great (540–604) described paintings of the lives of the saints as books that could be read by the illiterate; but today, most people can now only understand the pictures with the help of books.

right: St Agnes, Charles Landelle, *Les Saintes Femmes*, 19th century, French
The saint is quickly identified by two symbols — the lamb, which echoes her name, and the palm frond in her hand which symbolizes martyrdom.

Interview with Father Andrew Louth

Priest of the Russian Orthodox Patriarchal Diocese of Sourozh

What is the role of the saints in the life of an Orthodox Christian?

They play a large and obvious part in the lives of Orthodox Christians. The Mother of God and the saints are invoked at any celebration of the Divine Liturgy; all litanies end with an invocation of the saints. We venerate the relics of the saints, which are present on the holy table (or altar) during celebrations of the Divine Liturgy, sewn into a piece of cloth called an antimension.

Devotion to the saints is a normal part of Orthodox life: it is perfectly natural to treat them as friends, and as with human friends, some of them are special to us—perhaps those who we are named after, or those who we have come to know through their writings.

Reading those writings and the lives of the saints is a prominent part of our spiritual life. These saints are not just people from the remote past, there are also more recent ones such as Mother Maria Skobtsova, who was murdered by the Nazis, the ascetic, St. Siluan the Athonite, and Father Arseny, who although not yet formally canonized, is very much regarded as a saint.

What is the procedure for the canonization of saints in the Orthodox Church?

Canonization is the privilege of a patriarchate: the decision to declare a person a saint is made by one of the patriarchs on the advice of his Holy Synod. In practice, saints canonized by one patriarch are recognized in the other patriarchates, too. The procedure is nothing like as elaborate as that followed in the Roman Catholic Church.

What is the significance of icons in the Orthodox cult of the saints?

Icons mark out the frontiers between this world and the next, in which the saints who are very much alive are our friends in the kingdom of Heaven. There is no mystique about "praying with icons," as if it were some kind of technique. There are icons in churches which are venerated by Orthodox Christians, who kiss them and burn candles before them: it is a way of greeting the saints they depict, of reminding ourselves of their presence. In Orthodox homes, there will be an "icon corner," with a lamp or candle burning, as a place of prayer. Again, the idea is that the icons remind us that in prayer we join with the saints.

Author's notes

Mother Maria Skobtsova (1891–1945) nun who worked tirelessly for outcasts and exiles, ultimately in occupied Paris, where she was arrested for helping and rescuing Jews. Sent to Ravensbrück concentration camp, she continued to offer love and encouragement to all around her until her death.

St. Siluan the Athonite (1866–1938) visionary Russian monk of Mount Athos, who wrote with simplicity and urgency on the need for humility and the love of one's enemies.

Father Arseny (1893–1973) saintly survivor of Stalin's persecution of the church. He spent thirty-nine years in the gulag, where he was seen by fellow prisoners as the living embodiment of prayer and hope.

Interview with The Rt Rev. Richard Harries DD FKC FRSL

Bishop of Oxford

What is the role of the saints in the life of an Anglican Christian?

It varies greatly from church to church because Anglicanism encompasses both Calvinists and Catholics. At the Protestant end of Anglicanism, the saints are seen simply as exemplars; at the Catholic end, they are regarded in exactly the same way as in the Roman Catholic Church, and looked to for support, addressed in prayers, and mentioned in the liturgy. In the middle, "Broad Church" Anglicans consider the saints to be more than mere exemplars, and the doctrine of the Communion of Saints has an important place in the writings of Anglican divines.

What is the procedure for including saints in the Anglican calendar?

People are not formally "canonized" as they are in the Roman Catholic Church: they are included in the calendar by acclaim, as was the ancient custom. Names that are put forward are considered by the liturgical committee, and its proposals are then voted on by General Synod.

Who are the Anglican saints?

We have a calendar of saints that is very encompassing: it includes pre-reformation saints, of course, but it also commemorates a good number of later saints of the Church of England. So as well as universal saints like John the Baptist and English ones like Alban and Ethelreda, we include people such as John Bunyan, Josephine Butler, Dr Johnson, William Law, Archbishop Luwum, Henry Martyn, and William Wilberforce.

What is it that makes these people not just good, but saints?

It is their Christian commitment, the role they play in the life of the church and the recognition that they are not just good citizens or social reformers, but that all their work has been activated and motivated by their Christian faith. What sets a saint apart from everybody else is personal holiness; I think that a person can be an outstanding Christian without necessarily being a saint. You can be a saint having lived quite an obscure life; obviously, it is the people who lead more prominent lives who tend to come to the attention of the church, but I think—and I hope—that there are many more unknown saints than the ones that we know about.

Author's notes

John Bunyan (1628–88) lay preacher who earned his living as a tinker; imprisoned for preaching without a license, he wrote the spiritual classic *The Pilgrim's Progress*, an allegory of a Christian's pilgrimage through this world to the Celestial City that is his heavenly home.

Josephine Butler (1828–1906) defender of downtrodden women and campaigner against the Contagious Diseases Act, a law that was passed to ensure a supply of disease-free prostitutes for the military, and which reduced many women to sexual slavery.

Samuel Johnson (1709–84) best known as the compiler of the first dictionary of the English language, he was a man of magnanimity and piety, who composed prayers of great spiritual and literary beauty.

William Law (1686–1761) priest and author of *A Serious Call To a Devout and Holy Life*, a book whose call to love God was answered by many, including Samuel Johnson, William Wilberforce, and John and Charles Wesley.

Janani Luwum (1922–77) martyr; Archbishop of Uganda, murdered for daring to rebuke the tyrant Idi Amin for his atrocities against the Ugandan people and church.

Henry Martyn (1781–1812) missionary, who translated the New Testament into Hindi and Persian, the psalms into Persian and the Prayer Book into Hindi. His diary is considered a devotional treasury.

William Wilberforce (1759–83) Member of Parliament who devoted much of his life to the abolition of the slave trade; he called it an affront to "conscience, the principles of justice and the law of God." A year after he died, all slaves in the British Empire were set free.

At the Last Judgment I shall not be asked if I was successful in my ascetic exercises or how many prostrations I made in the course of my prayers. I shall be asked, did I feed the hungry, clothe the naked, visit the sick and the prisoners: that is all I shall be asked.

MOTHER MARIA SKOBTSOVA

The soul cannot know peace unless she prays for her enemies.

ST. SILUAN THE ATHONITE

I see no business in life but the work of Christ.

HENRY MARTYN

In this world, you must walk the paths of God's commandments: be merciful to one another; in your behavior and actions try to be like monks—even though you live in this stormy sea of life.

FATHER ARSENY

O GOD, grant me to resolve aright, and to keep my resolutions, for Jesus Christ's sake. Amen

SAMUEL JOHNSON

Love and pity and wish well to every soul in the world; dwell in love, and then you dwell in God.

WILLIAM LAW

chapter 2

Apostles and Disciples

The Evangelists

The stories of the first Christian saints are told in the New Testament, which was itself written by saints. The authors of the four gospels are known as the Evangelists: SS. Matthew, Mark, Luke, and John. The other books of the New Testament are the Acts of the Apostles, written by St. Luke, and Epistles by SS. Paul, James, Peter, Jude, and St. John, who also wrote the Book of Revelation, or Apocalypse.

The gospels tell the story of the life, teachings, death, and resurrection of Jesus. Acts relates the early history of the church. The Epistles are letters to individual Christian communities and to Christians in general, explaining Christ's teachings and exhorting people to follow them. The Apocalypse is a work of visionary prophecy. It uses poetic imagery to describe the church, its relationship with the pagan world, and its final triumph.

The gospel that bears Matthew's name is traditionally attributed to Matthew the Apostle, but some now doubt this. St. Matthew is called "Levi" in the Gospels of Mark and Luke. He was a Jew, but worked for the Romans as a tax collector, a profession that his countrymen can only have regarded with contempt. Little is known about the later years of his life, and there are conflicting accounts of the time, place and manner of his death. It is generally accepted that he was martyred.

previous page: **The Last Supper, Giotto, 1266–1377, Italian**
It was at this gathering of the Apostles that Jesus instituted the central act of Christian worship, the Eucharist.
right: **St. Matthew, Guido Reni, 1575–1642, Italian**
St. Matthew writes his gospel with the help of an angel.

St. Mark

A little more is known about St. Mark (d. c. 74), who is believed to be the boy who followed Jesus into the garden of Gethsemane and ran away when he was arrested. The event is described in the fourteenth chapter of his gospel. Most scholars identify him as the son of Mary of Jerusalem, whose house was used by the disciples as a meeting place. He was a cousin of St. Barnabas, with whom he preached in Cyprus. Mark worked closely with St. Peter, who referred to him affectionately as his "son." Little of Mark's later life is known for certain, but one source describes him as being the first bishop of Alexandria, and tradition says that he was martyred under Nero. In about 828, Mark's relics were moved to Venice, where his emblem—a winged lion—became the symbol of the city itself.

**Untir'd she read the legend page
Of holy Mark, from youth to age,
On land, on sea, in pagan chains,
Rejoicing for his many pains.**

JOHN KEATS, *THE EVE OF ST. MARK*

left: **St. Mark, *Book of Hours,* Simon Marmion c.1425–89, French**
St. Mark writes his gospel accompanied by his identifying emblem, a lion.

St. Luke

St Luke's idiomatic language and his early biographers identify him as Greek. He was a doctor. St Paul refers to him in his Epistle to the Colossians (4: 14) as "the beloved physician." We know from Acts— which Luke wrote—that he accompanied Paul on several of his missionary journeys. His gospel is written for the benefit of the gentiles: he carefully translates any Hebrew terms he uses, and is less concerned with Jesus' fulfilment of Old Testament prophecies (with which only Jews would have been familiar) than with his message of salvation for the whole world.

Luke's writings suggest an attractive, gentle character. His gospel emphasizes the loving-kindness and compassion of Jesus. Only Luke records his words of comfort to the women of Jerusalem during his passion (23: 27–31), and his promise to the repentant thief who was crucified beside him (23: 42–43):

And he said unto Jesus, Lord, remember me when thou comest into thy kingdom. And Jesus said unto him, Verily I say unto thee, Today shalt thou be with me in paradise.

It is Luke who reports the parable of the Prodigal Son (15: 11–32), who is welcomed with affection as well as forgiveness on his return: "But when he was yet a great way off, his father saw him, and had compassion, and ran, and fell on his neck, and kissed him." Luke gives more prominence than the other evangelists to women. He alone mentions Mary's cousin, Elizabeth (1: 5–66), the widow of Nain, whose son Jesus restores to life (7: 11–17), as well as the woman who was a sinner, who anointed Jesus' feet and dried them with her hair (7: 37–50). Luke is the only evangelist to tell the story of the Annunciation, and it is his gospel that gives us the Magnificat and the central words of the "Hail Mary" prayer. He clearly had a particular admiration and affection for the Virgin Mary; an ancient tradition asserts that he painted her portrait. Icons once attributed to him have been shown to be of later date, but it is at least possible that they could be copies—or copies of copies—of a lost original.

**My soul doth magnify the Lord,
And my spirit hath rejoiced in God my Saviour.
For he hath regarded the low estate of his handmaiden: for, behold, from henceforth all generations shall call me blessed.
For he that is mighty hath done to me great things; and holy is his name.
And his mercy is on them that fear him from generation to generation.**

LUKE 1: 46–50

next page: **St. Luke Drawing the Madonna, Rogier van der Weyden, c. 1399–1464, Dutch**
The tradition that St. Luke painted the Virgin makes him a patron saint of artists.

St. John

The tradition that identifies the author of St. John's gospel as St. John the Apostle is ancient, but disputed. St. John was the son of Zebedee and the brother of St. James. Jesus called John and James "sons of thunder," a description that suggests a fiery temperament. John is also described as "the disciple Jesus loved." He was the only Apostle present at Christ's trial and at the foot of the cross, from which Jesus asked him to take care of his mother. During the persecutions against Christians ordered by the emperor Domitian, he lived in exile on the Greek island of Patmos, where he wrote the Book of Revelation with its astounding visions and prophecies:

John, your brother and your partner in tribulation, and in the kingdom, and patience in Christ Jesus, was in the island, which is called Patmos, for the word of God, and for the testimony of Jesus.

APOCALYPSE 1: 9

right: St. John on the Isle of Patmos, *Book of Hours*, Simon Marmion, c. 1425–89, French
The presence of an eagle identifies the subject as St. John.

The Disciples

The main character in the history recorded by the four Evangelists is Jesus, but they also tell us something of his family and his disciples. The twelve main disciples are called the Apostles, and they are all known as "saints" except for Judas Iscariot, who betrayed Jesus, despaired of salvation, and hanged himself. After his suicide, his place was taken by St. Matthias, of whom hardly anything is known.

The twelve Apostles are named in Matthew's gospel (10: 2–4) as follows: Simon called Peter, Andrew (his brother), James and John (the sons of Zebedee), Philip, Bartholomew, Matthew, James (son of Alphaeus), Thaddeus (also called Jude), Simon Zelotes, Thomas Didymus ("Thomas the twin") and Judas Iscariot. They were all present at the Last Supper; they all (except Judas) witnessed Christ's Ascension into Heaven, and were gathered together when the Holy Spirit descended on them at Pentecost. Paintings of the Apostles usually show twelve (generally with six either side of Jesus) although after the conversion of St. Paul, there were thirteen until the martyrdom of St. James. To preserve the symmetry, Matthias is usually left out.

And they went forth, and preached everywhere, the Lord working with them, and confirming the word with signs following.

MATTHEW 16: 20

The original name of St. Peter (d. c. 64) was Simon. He and his brother St. Andrew (d. c. 60) were fishermen from Bethsaida, a town on Lake Genasareth. We know that Peter was married, because Matthew's and Luke's Gospels record that he lived with his mother-in-law in Capharnaum. St. Clement of Alexandria (c. 150–215) writes that Peter had children, and says that his wife suffered martyrdom.

When Andrew introduced his brother Simon to Jesus, he told him that from that moment on he would be called *Cephas*, which is the Aramaic form of "Peter," a name that is close both in that language and in Latin to the word for "rock." The significance was explained later, when Jesus told Peter that he was the rock upon which his church would be built, and that he would be given "the keys of the kingdom of heaven." Crossed keys thus figure in the coats of arms of the popes, Peter's successors as leaders of the church.

The work of St. Peter in Jerusalem, Judaea, and as far north as Syria is described the Acts of the Apostles. He was the leader of the Christian community and made many of the decisions that shaped the future of the church. He was the first of the Apostles to perform a public miracle, curing a lame man at the Beautiful Gate of the temple. Peter was imprisoned during the persecution of Christians by the king of Judea, Herod Agrippa, during which St. James was martyred.

Had Peter not miraculously escaped—Acts describes how he was visited by an angel, and the chains fell from his wrists—he would have been put to death then, too. His own martyrdom came after a period of missionary work in Rome, where he was executed under Nero, by being crucified upside down.

St. Peter

Peter was a man of action—at times, to the point of impetuosity: he drew a sword and cut off the ear of one of the men sent to arrest Jesus. He also knew fear: accused of being a Christian after Jesus had been taken, he three times denied it. The bitterness of his regret at his betrayal is vividly expressed in Matthew's Gospel. The very human picture that emerges from the New Testament is complemented by the traditional description of Peter's physical appearance. From the earliest paintings of the Apostles onward, Peter is shown as having short curly hair, a beard, and strong features.

left: **The Denial of St. Peter, Rembrandt van Rijn, 1606–69, Dutch**
Peter was a great leader despite this moment of weakness.

St. Paul

The second-century Apocryphal Acts of St. Paul (d. c. 65). describe him as "a man of little stature, thin haired upon the head, crooked in the legs, of good state of body, with eyebrows joining and nose somewhat hooked." Whether or not this picture is accurate, most images in art show him partly bald, with a high forehead. There is no uncertainty about his forceful personality however. Originally named Saul, Paul was a Jewish tent-maker from Tarsus. He was also an enthusiastic persecutor of Christians, and was one of those who watched St. Stephen stoned to death. His conversion to Christianity occurred dramatically, when he was suddenly struck blind on the road to Damascus.

After recovering his sight, he was baptized, spent three years in solitude, and then began to preach the gospel with great energy. He traveled widely and tirelessly—his journeys totaled some 8,000 miles (13,000 km.) He describes some of the difficulties he endured in his *Second Letter to the Corinthians*, in which he writes that he was flogged, beaten with rods, stoned, and was shipwrecked three times, once spending a day and a night in the water.

Paul's missionary work was remarkable, but he also contributed greatly to the development of Christian theology. His *Epistles* were more than mere exhortations: they outlined an understanding of the nature of Redemption upon which later theologians were to build.

right: **The Apostles St. Peter and St. Paul, El Greco, 1541–1614, Spanish**
Paul is on the right. The two saints are regarded as twin pillars of the church.

SS. James the Apostles

St. James the Greater (d. 44) is given that title to distinguish him from the other Apostle called James, who is known as James the Less. What we know of James the Greater from the gospels is that he was present with his brother John and St. Peter at the Transfiguration, when they saw Moses and Elijah talking to Jesus, whose "face did shine as the sun, and his raiment was white as the light" (Matthew 2: 17). James was also with Jesus in the garden of Gesthemene. He was the first of the Apostles to be martyred—he was put to death by Herod Agrippa. The story that he visited Spain and that his body was miraculously returned there is the origin of the great pilgrimage of Santiago de Compostela. In art, James is usually dressed as a pilgrim with his identifying emblem of the scallop shell.

As for St. James the Less (d. 62), the son of Alphaeus, very little is known about him except that he was sentenced by the Jewish court, the Sanhedrin, to be stoned to death. It is not certain whether he was the same person as James "the brother of the Lord," who saw the risen Christ and is often referred to as the first bishop of Jerusalem. He might possibly have been the James whose mother stood at the foot of the cross. He is sometimes identified in art with a fuller's mallet or club, the implement which his legend says was used to deliver the *coup de grâce* at his martyrdom.

left: **St. James the Greater, Alonso Cano, 1601–67, Spanish**
The saint is usually represented as a pilgrim; here, he carries a pilgrim's staff.

St. Philip

St. Philip, like SS. Peter and Andrew, came from Bethsaida in Galilee. It was Philip who persuaded Nathanael (St. Bartholomew) to join the disciples. We catch a glimpse of his personality at the famous incident of the feeding of the five thousand when Jesus asked "Whence shall we buy bread, that these may eat?" Philip answered, "Two hundred pennyworth of bread is not sufficient for them." It was Philip who, at the Last Supper, asked Jesus to show them the Father, prompting his declaration that "The person who has seen me has seen my Father also." The story of Philip's later life is obscure, and there is some historical confusion with the deacon called Philip the Evangelist. It is no longer thought to be certain that Philip the Apostle was martyred, but images of St. Philip often include a cross.

Philip findeth Nathanael, and saith unto him, We have found him, of whom Moses in the law, and the prophets, did write, Jesus of Nazareth, the son of Joseph.

JOHN 1:45

left: **St. Philip the Apostle, engraving, unnamed**
Little is known about St. Philip, but he is believed to have preached in Phrygia and to have been martyred at Hierapolis.

St. Bartholomew

"Bartholomew" is a surname, meaning "son of Tolmai," and most scholars now believe that St. Bartholomew is the same person as the disciple known by the first name, Nathanael. When St. Philip told Bartholomew that they had found Jesus, he responded "Can any good come out of Nazareth?" to which Philip's reply was "Come and see." The brief exchange suggests a directness of speech, but we have few other clues to Bartholomew's character, except that when he did meet Jesus, he believed in him immediately. According to the historian Eusebius, when St. Pantaenus (d. c. 190) visited India in the latter half of the second century, he found a copy of St. Matthew's Gospel that had been left behind by St. Bartholomew. Tradition says that Bartholomew was martyred by being flayed alive and then beheaded, and images of the saint often include the knife used in his torture. Perhaps the best-known picture of him is his figure in Michelangelo's *Last Judgment*, which shows him carrying his own skin.

Bartholomew preached to men of India, and delivered to them the gospel after Matthew in their proper tongue.

THE GOLDEN LEGEND

right: **St. Bartholomew with his Flayed Skin, Michelangelo Buonarroti, 1475–1564, Italian**
The face on the saint's flayed skin is that of the artist.

St. Jude

St. Jude, who is believed to be the same person as Thaddeus, is the author of the Epistle of St. Jude. Not much more is known about him than that. The apocryphal Passion of Simon and Jude describes the two saints preaching the gospel in Persia, where they were martyred. The basic facts of this account are accepted as true. St. Jude is traditionally regarded as the patron saint of lost causes, possibly because his name is so like that of Judas, whose final sin was one of despair. St. Jude shares his feast day (June 28th) with St. Simon Zelotes, about whom little more is known—though his name suggests that he was once a member of the strict Jewish sect, the Zealots.

... it was needful for me to write unto you, and exhort you that ye should earnestly contend for the faith which was once delivered unto the saints.

JUDE 1: 3

left: Thaddaus or St. Jude, James Tissot, 1836–1902, French
St. Jude's writings suggest he was a powerful preacher.

Except I shall see in his hands the print of the nails, and put my finger into the print of the nails, and thrust my hand into his side, I will not believe.

JOHN 20: 25

left: **The Doubting Thomas**
Alessandro Mantovani,
1814–92, Italian
The cure of his spiritual blindness makes St. Thomas a patron of the physically blind.

89

St. Thomas

The gospels give a vivid picture of St. Thomas; he was called "Didymus," the Greek word for "twin," though nothing is said about who his twin might have been. Thomas appears in three main episodes. He confidently offers to die with Jesus on the way to Bethany (John 11: 16), but in his other two appearances, he expresses doubt. When, after the Last Supper, Jesus tells the Apostles, "I go and prepare a place for you, I will come again, and receive you unto myself; that where I am, there ye may be also. And whither I go ye know, and the way ye know," it is Thomas who asks, "Lord, we know not whither thou goest; and how can we know the way?" (John. 14:5). After the Resurrection, he flatly refused to believe that Jesus has risen from the dead until he is able to touch his wounds with his own hands. When he did so, he explicitly confessed his belief in Christ's Divinity in the words, "My Lord and my God." This last incident has been frequently depicted in art. There is uncertainty about Thomas' later work as an Apostle, but tradition and several early apocryphal "acts" and "gospels" of St. Thomas assert that he preached in India, where he was martyred.

Come, O Apostle, and feel the palms in which they fastened the nails. O good unbelief of Thomas, which hath led the hearts of the faithful to knowledge!

ORTHODOX VESPERS OF ST. THOMAS SUNDAY

The Holy Family

The immediate members of Jesus' family have always been regarded as saints, and his mother, the Blessed Virgin Mary, is considered the greatest saint of all. Her husband, St. Joseph, is mentioned in the gospels of Matthew and Luke, but nothing is said about her parents. They appear in apocryphal texts including the second-century *Gospel of James*, which identify them as SS. Joachim and Anne. The emperor Justinian (d. 565) built a church dedicated to St. Anne in Constantinople, and there are relics and eighth-century pictures of her In the church of S. Maria Antiqua in Rome.

The cult of St. Joachim seems to have started later and has been less constant, focusing on his role as a husband to his more famous wife. Medieval legends supplied sufficient imaginary details to bring them both alive as individual characters. *The Golden Legend* includes the invention that Anne married twice after Joachim's death, gave the name "Mary" to the daughter she had by each, and that these two Marys produced a number of cousins for Jesus, including several who were to become his Apostles. Such stories are obvious fictions.

They were invented to satisfy a desire to get nearer to the characters who were close to the historical Jesus, and that way, to get nearer to him. Medieval paintings of scenes from these legends, or of St. Anne holding Mary on her lap and teaching her to sew or read reflect a profound tenderness felt toward the Blessed Virgin, and her role as a mother to her divine Son.

St. Joseph

A descendent of King David, Joseph lived in Nazareth, where he worked as a carpenter. The Bible does not tell us his age, but tradition and early apocryphal writings make him considerably older than Mary, which emphasizes that he is not the physical father of Jesus, who was conceived by the power of the Holy Spirit. His character emerges as one of honorable and kindly protectiveness. He was betrothed to the Virgin Mary, but when he learned that she was pregnant, but not by him, he resolved not to marry her. His mind was changed when an angel appeared to him in a dream. Similar guidance moved him to take Mary and Jesus away to escape Herod's massacre of all newborn babies; their journey of escape was frequently painted under the title "The flight into Egypt." Again, an angel told him when it was safe to return. Joseph drops out of the gospel story after the twelve-year-old Jesus was found preaching in the temple.

**"Joseph dearest, Joseph mine,
Help me cradle the child divine;
God reward thee and all that's thine
In paradise," so prays the mother, Mary.**

GERMAN MYSTERY PLAY, C. 1500

right: **Madonna with the Beardless Joseph, Raphael, 1483–520, Italian**
Departing from tradition, the artist depicts St. Joseph without a beard.

Devotion to St. Joseph suffered something of a setback in the Middle Ages. It became customary to play his part for laughs in the popular mystery plays, and a number of paintings of the period show him as a doddering old character. A more positive view of him was encouraged by later saints, most particularly St. Teresa of Avila (1512–82), who put the mother-house of her reformed Carmelite convents under his patronage. Pope Pius IX awarded him the title "Patron of the Universal Church" in 1870; in 1956, Pius XII made the humble carpenter a patron of all human work by establishing the feast of St. Joseph the Worker. The date chosen for this feast was May 1st—a direct challenge to the May Day festivals celebrated in atheistic communist countries. In 1962, Pope John XXIII added Joseph's name to the list of saints mentioned in the ancient Canon of the mass. The growth in his popularity is reflected in the scope of his patronage. He is the patron saint not only of tradesmen and workers, but also of travelers and refugees, the persecuted, Christian homes and families, those engaged to be married, the homeless, the poor, the old, the sick, and the dying.

Joseph shines among all mankind by the most august dignity, since by divine will he was the guardian of the Son of God

ENCYCLICAL OF POPE LEO XIII, *QUANQUAM PLURIES*

Mary, Mother of Jesus

What we know for sure about the life of the Virgin Mary is found in the New Testament. St. Luke devotes much of the first two chapters of his gospel to her, and she is referred to significantly but infrequently in the gospels of Matthew, John, and Mark, and in the *Acts of the Apostles*. These references relate how Mary was betrothed to Joseph, told by the Angel Gabriel that she was to bear the Messiah, and visited St. Elizabeth, the mother of John the Baptist. She gave birth to Jesus, was visited by shepherds and wise men, presented her infant Son in the Temple, fled to Egypt to avoid Herod's massacre of new babies, and found her twelve-year-old Son preaching in the temple. She asked Jesus to perform his first miracle at the marriage feast at Cana and went to hear him preach. She stood at the foot of his cross on Calvary and was with the Apostles in the upper room at Pentecost.

Taken together, these fragments amount to little more than a basic biography, and they tell nothing of Mary's early life or her death. But it is their significance rather than their quantity that is important. When early theologians such as St. Irenaeus of Lyons (c. 130–200) began to ponder on Christ's divinity and humanity, they realized that the part played by his mother in the world's redemption was central and unique. In 431 this teaching was confirmed by the Council of Ephesus. The fact that Mary had maintained her virginity perpetually had already been taught by church fathers including St. Ambrose (339–97) and St. Hilary of Poitiers (c. 315–68). Later, St. Gregory of Tours (539–94) and St. John Damascene (c. 657–749) formulated the ancient belief that Mary's uncorrupted body had been assumed into Heaven. Belief that Mary was born without the stain of Original Sin is equally ancient.

Both doctrines were formally defined much later. Pope Pius IX (who was beatified in 2000) proclaimed the doctrine of the Immaculate Conception in 1854; Pope Pius XII did the same for the Assumption in 1950. The special veneration owed to Mary—higher than that owed to the other saints, but lower than the honor owed to God, which is worship (*latria*)—had been defined (as *hyperdulia*) by St. Thomas Aquinas (c.1225–74).

Behind these intellectual and theological considerations lies one simple truth that makes Mary preeminent among the saints and the object of particular devotion. She is the mother of Jesus. No human being could ever be as close to him as the woman in whose womb he grew, who gave birth to him, who nursed him, and who nurtured him as a child. Nobody else could possibly have loved him with the particular tenderness of a mother for a son. Nobody else could possibly have felt the unique sorrow of watching that son cruelly put to death. But every person who has ever been born has had a mother, and everyone can imagine how intense Mary's love and suffering must have been.

Stabat Mater dolorosa
iuxta Crucem lacrimosa,
dum pendebat Filius.

JACAPONE DA TODI

At the cross her station keeping,
stood the mournful mother weeping,
close to Jesus to the last.

METRICAL VERSION BY FR. EDWARD CASWALL

Images of the Virgin

Appreciation of the Virgin Mary was widely expressed in art as well as writing. The few surviving representations of her in paintings in the Catacombs do not give her unusual prominence, but by the time that the fifth-century Council of Ephesus approved the title *Theotokos* ("Mother of God"), images asserting that status had begun to appear. In these, Mary holds Jesus in her arms or on her lap, but their expressions are solemn, rather than intimate. These pictures assert a truth that had been recently challenged—that Mary's baby is both the true God and a true man. Another traditional icon that asserts a particular teaching is the "Virgin Hodegtria," named after the original in the Hodegon monastery. It shows Mary holding Jesus in her left arm and pointing to him with her right. She is indicating that he alone is the way to salvation.

As early challenges to the doctrine of the Incarnation faded, representations of the Madonna and Child became much more humanized. Their expressions softened, and they were shown looking lovingly at each other, rather than assertively and outwardly at the world. Icon painters in the East began to show the mother touching her cheek to that of her child, who puts his arm around her neck. The full divinity of Christ was no longer disputed. His humanity could be shown with affectionate confidence, especially in his relationship with his mother.

By the seventh century, these images influenced portrayals of the Madonna and Child in the West. Early medieval Western art shows the Virgin as *Sedes Sapientiae* ("Seat of Wisdom"). She is seated on a regal throne, with Jesus on her lap; his kingship of creation and her queenship of Heaven are indicated by crowns. By the later Middle Ages, less formal and more human representations were back in fashion.

At morn, at noon, at twilight dim,
Maria, thou hast heard my hymn:
In joy and woe, in good and ill,
Mother of God, be with me still

EDGAR ALLAN POE

right: **The Virgin with the Veil, 1515, Raphael, Italian**
The Madonna shows the sleeping Christ-child to his cousin, St. John.

Lullay, my liking, my dear son,
   my sweeting
Lullay, my dear heart, mine
   own dear darling

MEDIEVAL CAROL

left: **Madonna and Child with the Saints Ansano, Antonio, Girolamo, and Francesco, Bartolomeo Montagna, c. 1450–1525, Italian**
The formal pose is softened by the physical contact between mother and child.

Mary's Life is enriched by apocryphal early sources such as the *Protoevangelium* of St. James. Later versions were augmented by medieval legends of the saints. The composite biography includes details of Mary's birth, childhood, marriage, death, and her assumption into and coronation in Heaven. These events are sometimes depicted in sequences of paintings, sometimes individually. Mary's sufferings at and after the Crucifixion have inspired some of the world's greatest art, such as the *Pietà* of Michelangelo (1475–1564).

Ah! Mary, pierced with sorrow,
Remember, reach and save
The soul that comes tomorrow
Before the God that gave!
Since each was born of woman,
For each at utter need,
True comrade and true foeman—
Madonna, intercede!

RUDYARD KIPLING

right: **Mary Queen of Heaven, Master of the St. Lucy Legend,**
15th century, Dutch
Singing angels hold the score of the hymn Ave Regina (Hail, Queen of Heaven).

Angels and Archangels
May have gathered there,
Cherubim and seraphim
Thronged the air,
But only His mother
In her maiden bliss
Worshipped the Belovèd
With a kiss.

CHRISTINA ROSSETTI, *IN THE BLEAK MID-WINTER*

Of a certainty, O Jesus, Son of God, and
thou, O Mother Mary, you desire that
whatever you love should be loved by us.
Therefore, O good Son, I beg thee, by the
love thou bearest Thy Mother, and as Thou
wishest her to be loved, to grant to me that
I may truly love her.

ST. ANSELM

By the grace of God, if we always keep in mind the acts and words of the Blessed Mary, we shall always persevere in the observance of the works of a pure and virtuous life.

THE VENERABLE BEDE

He came also still
There his Mother lay
As dew in April
That falleth on the spray.

MEDIEVAL CAROL, *I SING OF A MAIDEN THAT IS MAKELESS,*

Hail, Mary, of all things in the whole world most precious. Hail, Mary, dove undefiled. Hail, Mary, inextinguishable lamp; for of thee is born the Sun of Justice. Hail, Mary, the place of Him who is not held by place.

ST. CYRIL OF ALEXANDRIA

John the Baptist

John the Baptist was the son of Zachariah, a priest of the Temple, and of Elizabeth, a cousin of the Virgin Mary. Elizabeth believed herself too old to have children, but the Archangel Gabriel told her that she would give birth to a son, whom she should call John. When he was about twenty-seven, he went to live in the desert, where he lived on what little food he could find—a diet of honey and locusts—and began his mission to proclaim the coming of the Messiah.

Among those he baptized was Christ himself, whom he recognized when he saw the Holy Spirit descend on him "like a dove." John denounced Herod for his immoral marriage to his niece, Herodias. She and her daughter, Salome, had their revenge when Herod, entranced by Salome's dancing, offered her anything she might want. She asked for the head of John the Baptist, and it was presented to her on a dish.

And he sent, and beheaded John in the prison. And his head was brought in a charger, and given to the damsel: and she brought it to her mother.

MATTHEW 14: 10–11

left: **St. John the Baptist, Leonardo da Vinci, 1452–1519, Italian**
Leonardo's John the Baptist is not the usual lean and gaunt figure.

St. Mary Magdalene

St. Mary Magdalene is mentioned by name in all four gospels. We are told that she was a disciple of Jesus, and that he had released seven devils from her; that she was present at his crucifixion, and that she recognized him after his resurrection. St. Gregory the Great (c. 540–604) identified her with the unnamed "woman which was a sinner" who washed and anointed Jesus' feet at the house of a Pharisee (Luke 7: 37), and also with Mary of Bethany, the sister of Martha and Lazarus. This makes her a model of devotion and repentance, which is how she is traditionally represented in art. She is usually depicted with a pot of ointment. The eastern church has always considered these three characters to be different people, and venerates Mary of Bethany and Mary Magdalene as separate saints. In 1969, the Roman Catholic church separated the characters in its revised missal. Today, the church regards Mary Magdalene as more important for being the first to see the risen Christ, a privilege that is seen as a reward for her wholehearted devotion. Her loyalty led her to witness his crucifixion, after which she stood weeping at his tomb believing his body to have been taken away.

… and weeping Magdalene,
Who in the penitential desert met
Gales sweet as those that over Eden blew!

WILLIAM WORDSWORTH, *ECCLESIASTICAL SONNETS, XXIV*

left: **St. Mary Magdalene Reading, Ambrosius Benson,
c. 1495–1550, Dutch**
The saint is identified by her pot of ointment in the foreground.

Now when Jesus was risen early the first day of the week, he appeared first to Mary Magdalene, out of whom he had cast seven devils. And she went and told them that had been with him, as they mourned and wept. And they, when they had heard that he was alive, and had been seen of her, believed not.

MARK 16: 9-11

O three tymes happy twoe: O golden payre
Who with your bloode, dyd lay the churches ground

HENRY CONSTABLE, *TO ST. PETER AND ST. PAUL*

For as the body without the spirit is dead, so faith without works is dead also.

JAMES 2: 26

We love him, because he first loved us. If a man say, I love God, and hateth his brother, he is a liar: for he that loveth not his brother whom he hath seen, how can he love God whom he hath not seen? And this commandment have we from him, That he who loveth God love his brother also.

JOHN 4: 19-21

Love worketh no ill to his neighbor: therefore love is the fulfilling of the law.

ST. PAUL, ROMANS 13: 10

chapter 3

Persecutions and Asceticism

The Early Martyrs

In the three centuries before their religion was first officially tolerated by the emperor Constantine, Christians were persecuted sporadically. Sometimes, and in some places, that persecution was intense. The first episode was after the great fire in Rome in 64. People suspected that their mad emperor, Nero, had started it for his own perverted amusement; to divert public anger, he blamed the Christians. The Roman historian Tacitus describes what happened to them: "They were not just put to death, they were also mocked. Some were covered in the skins of beasts and torn to death by dogs; some were crucified, and others were set on fire to light up the night when daylight failed." Many were sought out and executed, including SS. Peter and Paul. Paul was a Roman citizen, and was therefore beheaded; Peter was crucified upside down at his own request.

The Christians were convenient scapegoats. The Romans believed that everyone had a duty to perform the rites of the state religion. The Christians would not join in, and their refusal was seen as disloyalty amounting to treason. They conducted their own, foreign rituals behind closed doors, which led to rumor and suspicion.

previous page: **Christian Martyrs in the Circus Maximus from The Christian Martyrs' Last Prayer, Jean-Léon Gérôme, 1824–1904, French**
Many early Christian martyrdoms provided public entertainment.
right: **The Crucifixion of St. Peter, Jean Fouquet, reproduced in _Oeuvre de Jehan Foucquet_, 1866–7, French**
St. Peter did not feel worthy to die in the same manner as his master.

Imperial Persecutions

Nero's persecution was not sustained. When it died down, Christians were left in peace until the last three years of the reign of Domitian (81–96), whose actions were motivated by political fears concerning his cousin, whom he suspected of Christian sympathies. Trajan (98–117) did not actively seek out Christians but ordered that they should be punished according to the law if they were brought before the authorities. Those who suffered included Pope Clement and St. Ignatius of Antioch, who was thrown to the lions in the Colosseum of Rome in 107. Under Hadrian (117–38) and Antoninus Pius (138–61) there was more toleration than repression.

Persecutions during the reign of Marcus Aurelius (161–80) led to the death of the first Christian philosopher, Justin Martyr (100–165). A record of his trial survives, as does a contemporary account of the pogrom at Lyons in 177. This is quoted in the *Ecclesiastical History* written later by Eusebius (260–340): "Not only were we excluded from public buildings, baths and markets, but even the mere appearance of any one of us was forbidden, in any place whatsoever." The Christians of Lyons were then "hooted at, struck, dragged about, plundered, stoned [and] hemmed in" by the "inflamed rabble" before being dragged off to prison. Their terrified servants were persuaded to accuse their masters of cannibalism, incest, "and of things it is not lawful either to speak or think, nor even to believe that any such things were ever done among men." They were interrogated under torture and executed.

Left: Pope Clement I, artist unknown

The saint is shown dressed as a medieval pope.

The Emperor Commodus (180–92) left the Christians in peace, but Septimus Severus (193–211) sought to limit their influence by forbidding conversion. Then, apart from a brief period of persecution in the first year of the reign of Maximinus Thrax (235–38), Christians were left alone until the short and fierce persecution of Decius (249–51).

Decius sought to restore order and authority throughout the empire by requiring all his subjects to sacrifice to the gods of the state. The penalty for refusal was death. Many Christians avoided it by buying a forged *libellus*, the document that certified that they had sacrificed. Many others renounced their faith. Martyrs under Decius include the pope St. Fabian, St. Babylas, bishop of Antioch, St. Mercurius, the Christian commander of Decius' army, and St. Agatha.

The emperor Valerian (253–60) issued edicts forbidding Christians to meet together and requiring clergy and laymen of high rank to sacrifice to the Roman gods. Among those executed as a result were the popes SS. Sixtus and Cornelius, and Cyprian, Bishop of Carthage. Valerian's successor, Gallienus, revoked his anti-Christian laws and Christians were left largely untroubled until the Great Persecution under Diocletian (284–305) and his junior emperor Galerius (293–311).

Hear, all of you, that I am a Christian. Here are your titles and your dignities. Take them back, for they will perish with every vanity in the world.

ST. MERCURIUS

right: 11th-century painting, from *Les Arts Somptuaires*, 1857–8, French St. Mercurius was a military hero, who was beheaded under the emperor Decius for refusing to sacrifice to pagan gods.

The Great Persecution

Eusebius describes how the Great Persecution began under Decius in March 303: "Imperial edicts were published ... ordering that the churches be razed to the ground, that the scriptures be destroyed by fire." The following year, "it was ordered that all the people without exception should sacrifice in the several cities and offer libations to the idols." Those who died included St. Januarius, later patron saint of Naples, and the 15-year old St. Pelagia of Antioch. SS. Cosmas and Damian were martyred at Cyrrhus in Syria, St. Anastasia at Syrmium in Jugoslavia, and St. Chrysogonus was beheaded in Aquileia. The teenage St. Agnes died in Rome, and St. Lucy at Syracuse. One of Diocletian's first victims in Palestine was St. Procopius, whose trial is recorded in detail by Eusebius. He laughed in the faces of the officials who invited him to sacrifice to the emperors.

After Diocletian's abdication, persecution was particularly fierce in the East, under Maximinus II. In 311 Galerius issued an edict of toleration in the East, and in 313 the emperors Constantine and Licinius jointly issued the Edict of Milan, legally recognizing Christianity and ordering religious toleration throughout the whole empire.

Christianity had survived persecution and been strengthened by it— a truth expressed by the theologian Tertullian (160–220) "The blood of the martyrs is the seed of the church." By the end of the Roman persecutions, the church was firmly rooted, as was the cult of the saints.

left: **The Beheading of SS. Cosmas and Damian, Fra Angelico, c. 1400–1455, Italian**
Legend says the brothers were executed with three companions.

SS. Perpetua and Felicity

Perpetua was twenty-two and had recently given birth when persecutions began in Carthage in 203. She was arrested with several others, including a slave girl, Felicity, who was heavily pregnant. Their story is recorded in the *Acts of SS. Perpetua and Felicity*. The first part is told in the voice of St. Perpetua herself.

"All those who were interrogated before me boldly proclaimed their faith in Jesus Christ. When it was my turn, my father immediately appeared with my child. He took me to one side, tenderly pleading with me to consider the misery I should bring to the innocent creature to which I had given life.

[The judge] Hilarian added his words to my father's: 'Will you not be moved by the gray hairs of the father you are going to make miserable,' he said, 'or by the tender innocence of the child that your death will make an orphan? Sacrifice for the prosperity of the emperor!'

'I will not do it,' I replied. 'Are you a Christian, then?' said Hilarian. I answered: 'Yes, I am.' My father attempted to drag me from the platform, but Hilarian commanded him to be beaten off. When they hit him with a stick, I felt as if I had been struck myself. I was so sad to see my father treated like that in his old age."

previous page: **Persecution of the First Christians, Giuseppe Mancinelli, 1813–75, Italian**
Christians were seen as outsiders disloyal to the state.
left: **Saint Perpetua, 19th-century lithograph, Louis Lassalle, French**
SS. Perpetua and Felicity were thrown to wild beasts for refusing to abandon their faith.

St. Perpetua continued her story: "Then the judge pronounced our sentence: we were condemned to be exposed to wild beasts ... I sent ... [for] my baby, which I was breast-feeding. My father refused to give it up. But God ordained that the child no longer needed to suck, and I was not troubled by my milk."

Eyewitnesses record the events that followed. Felicity gave birth to a daughter, and gave it to a Christian woman to adopt. On the day of execution, Perpetua and Felicity were put in the ring with a raging heifer. It tossed Perpetua fiercely then severely injured Felicity. Perpetua helped her to her feet and they both returned to the gate of the amphitheater, where Perpetua asked when she was going to face the beasts: she had been so rapt in ecstasy that she was unaware that she had already been attacked. The crowd roared for them all to be taken to the center of the arena to be despatched with swords; the martyrs exchanged a kiss of peace and the executioners fell to their work. The man appointed to kill Perpetua bungled the job. She died slowly.

Though beheaded, and crucified, and thrown to wild beasts, and chains, and fire, and all other kinds of torture, we do not give up our faith; but, the more such things happen, the more do others in larger numbers become faithful.

ST. JUSTIN MARTYR

St. Polycarp

Saint Polycarp (69–155) was bishop of Smyrna, in Asia Minor. He had been a disciple of St. John the Apostle. We know about his life from several reliable contemporary sources, and there is also an authentic account of his death at the age of eighty-six, *The Encyclical Epistle of the Church at Smyrna, Concerning the Martyrdom of St. Polycarp*. This describes how after watching a young Christian called Germanicus torn to pieces by wild animals, the crowd in the amphitheater cried out for Polycarp to be produced, too.

One of his servants revealed his whereabouts under torture, and men were sent to arrest him. When he was brought into the stadium, the crowd roared. The proconsul asked him to recite the formula "Away with the atheists!"—"atheists" meaning those who refuse to worship the Roman gods. Polycarp spoke the words while pointing at the crowd to indicate that it was they who were rejecting the true God. He was then asked to renounce Christ, and in response said:

I have served him for eighty-six years ... and he never did me any harm. How can I now blaspheme my King and my Savior?

When the crowd were told of his defiance, they cried out for a lion to be set upon him, but the Asiarch (the presiding Roman official) replied that it was not permitted, as the shows of wild beasts had formally ended. So the mob called for him to be burned alive. A pyre was built and lit, but the flames did not reach him, which Christian onlookers interpreted as a miracle. An executioner ended his life with a dagger.

Precious in the sight of the Lord is the death of his saints.

PSALM 116

All of us are naturally frightened of dying and the dissolution of our bodies, but remember this most startling fact: that those who accept the faith of the cross despise even what is normally terrifying, and for the sake of Christ cease to fear even death.

ST. ATHANASIUS

We command that Ignatius, who affirms that he carries about within him Him that was crucified, be bound by soldiers, and carried to the great city of Rome, there to be devoured by the beasts, for the gratification of the people.

SENTENCE PASSED BY THE EMPEROR TRAJAN
UPON ST. IGNATIUS OF ANTIOCH, C. 107

Let those who have refused to sacrifice to the gods and to yield to the command of the emperor be scourged, and led away to suffer the punishment of decapitation, according to the laws.

SENTENCE PASSED UPON ST. JUSTIN MARTYR AND COMPANIONS, C. 165

You have set yourself up as an enemy of the gods of Rome and our religious practices. You have been discovered as the author and leader of these heinous crimes, and will consequently be held forth as an example for all those who have followed you in your crime. By your blood the law shall be confirmed. It is decided that Cyprian should die by the sword.

SENTENCE PASSED UPON ST. CYPRIAN, 258

St. Pâcome.

Ste VERONIQUE DE MILAN.

Ascetics: The Desert Fathers

The Roman persecutions had established martyrdom as a glorious road to sainthood, but when those persecutions ended, that route was closed. By the time of Theodosius the Great (378–95), the Roman empire had become a Christian theocracy. The church was powerful, rich, and comfortable. Those who wanted to renounce the values of this world absolutely needed to find a different way to Heaven. Many did so by turning their back on the decadence of the city and following the example of St. Paul of Thebes (d. 345) and St. Antony of Egypt (251–356) by going off to live as hermits or anchorites in the desert.

This was an ancient idea: many prophets had spent much of their lives in the wilderness, and Jesus had prayed and fasted for forty days in the desert. The "desert fathers" (many of whom were women) separated themselves from society in order to get closer to God, and through mortification of their bodies they offered themselves as living sacrifices. They lived in absolute poverty, in caves or huts they made with their own hands. They were often visited by pilgrims looking for spiritual advice. As their numbers increased, they began to gather in particular places, establishing their cells close to hermits famous for their saintliness, following their example and seeking their guidance.

St. Pachomius (292–346) founded the first monastery in the modern sense of the word on the Island of Tabennae in 320. There, monks lived together under his rule, eating and worshipping in common.

left: St. Pachomius, 19th-century lithograph, *Vie des Saints*, unnamed artist, French
St. Pachomius, Greek founder of monastic communities.

St. Antony of Egypt

St. Antony was born at Coma in Upper Egypt. At the age of twenty, he sold all his possessions and devoted his life to asceticism. Between the ages of 35 and 55, he lived in absolute solitude. During this time, a number of disciples established themselves as his satellites, and in 306 he organized them into a loose community under his rule. In 311 he traveled to Alexandria to encourage the Christian community during the persecutions of Maximinus II, and in 355 he went there again to challenge the Arians, the heretics who taught that Jesus Christ was not truly divine. Apart from these two journeys, he continued to live as a hermit on the side of a mountain above the Red Sea, at what became the Der Mar Antonios monastery. (The buildings still stand today.) He arranged to be buried in an unmarked grave, but it was discovered in 561 and his remains were taken to Alexandria. St. Athanasius wrote a *Life* of St. Antony that greatly contributed to his popularity, recording his battles against various temptations sent by the devil. These have frequently been depicted in art as struggles with physical demons.

Whoever sits in solitude and is quiet has escaped from three wars: hearing, speaking, and seeing. Yet against one thing he must constantly battle: his own heart.

ST. ANTONY OF EGYPT

right: **The Temptation of St. Antony, David Teniers II, 1610–90, Flemish**
St. Antony's temptations are often represented in art as demons.

St. Jerome

St. Jerome (c. 341 – 420) is one of the small number of saints that have been designated Doctors (that is, teachers) of the Church. He had a remarkable talent for scholarship. Inspired in a dream to devote himself to religious rather than literary studies, he spent five years learning Hebrew in the Syrian desert, leading the life of a hermit. After ordination as a priest and a course of further studies, he was briefly employed as a secretary by the pope, St. Damasus. At Damasus' suggestion, Jerome embarked on the great work for which he is chiefly remembered, the translation of the Bible into Latin.

Jerome seems to have been an all-or-nothing character who threw himself wholeheartedly into his enthusiasms. He wrote fervently of the need for monks and nuns to lead lives of asceticism. His contributions to the theological debates of the times made him enemies as well as admirers. While in Rome, he acted as spiritual adviser to a group of devout widows including St. Paula (d. 404). False rumors about his relationship with the women were circulated by his enemies, and in 385 he moved to Bethlehem, where he founded a monastery and St. Paula founded a convent.

Jerome is frequently shown with a lion, commemorating a story in which he is said to have tamed one by removing a thorn from its paw.

left: **St. Jerome in the Desert, c. 1499, Pietro Vanucci Perugino, Italian**
Jerome holds a stone with which he beats his breast.
next page: **St. Jerome Brings the Lion Into the Monastery, Vittore Carpaccio, c. 1455–1526, Italian**
Monks flee from the lion that Jerome has tamed with his kindness.

St. Simeon Stylites

St. Simeon Stylites (390–459) was a shepherd's son who joined a monastery near Antioch but was thrown out because his mortifications were so extreme. He wore a rope tied so tightly around himself that it ate into his flesh and had to be surgically removed. Unsuited to communal living, he became a hermit. He built a rough enclosure on top of a mountain, where he chained himself to a rock. He then sought out even more solitude and suffering by building a nine-foot (3-meter) pillar and living on it. Word of this astonishing spectacle spread, and people came to see him, so he built another one, twice as high.

This only increased his reputation for sanctity, and with it the visitors. He doubled the height of his pillar again, with similar results. He finally built one 60 feet (80 meters) high, and remained on it for the last twenty years of his life, living on a platform about six feet square (half a square meter). The little food and drink he wanted was hauled up on a rope. Pilgrims and sightseers—including the Roman emperor, Theodosius—thronged to him from all over the world. The sermons Simeon preached to them were surprisingly balanced and gentle. The ruins of the church and monastery built beside his pillar can still be seen today.

**I drowned the whoopings of the owl with sound
Of pious hymns and psalms, and sometimes saw
An angel stand and watch me, as I sang.**

TENNYSON: *ST. SIMEON STYLITES*

left: **Saint Simeon Stylites, icon, 16th century, Cypriot**
The word *stylite* means a person who lives on a pillar.

Saintly Self-discipline

The desert fathers were not the only saints to practice extreme forms of self-denial. Many others have disciplined themselves in ways that would not be encouraged by spiritual directors today. St. Frances of Rome (1384—1440) wore a hair shirt and a horsehair girdle, which replaced the iron one that her confessor had ordered her to take off because it so damaged her flesh. She ate almost nothing, and drank only water— it is said, from a human skull. The Redemptorist lay brother St. Gerard Majella (1725–55) slept on a mattress of thistles and stones, wore a hair shirt, and fasted more or less constantly, sprinkling what little food he ate with bitter herbs so as not to enjoy the taste.

But the saints who were toughest on themselves are invariably most gentle to others. St. Frances worked tirelessly for the destitute of Rome, and was loved for her kindness by all she met. St. Gerard, too, was known for his generosity to the poor, and his disarming humility. St. Thomas More (1478–1535) wore the fine clothes of a Lord Chancellor—but underneath, he wore a hair shirt. He is one of the many saints that scourged themselves during private prayer. These secret penances did not diminish his sweetness of temperament; they sustained it. St. Catherine of Siena (1347?–80) fasted so obsessively that some now consider her to have been anorexic. But her self-denial gave her the spiritual strength of a mystic, a prophet and a saint.

right: **St. Catherine Invested with the Dominican Habit, Giovanni di Paolo, c. 1403–82/3**
Catherine chooses between joining orders founded by SS. Dominic, Augustine and Francis.

It is very much better for you to be one among a crowd of a thousand people and to possess a very little humility, than to be a man living in the cave of a hyena in pride.

ST. PACHOMIUS

Solitude is the best context for quietening the mind and unlearning falsehood. Seek out a place of solitude, where you can train your soul without interruption, nourishing your soul with thoughts of God.

ST. BASIL

Do not trust in your own righteousness do not worry about the past, but
control your tongue and your stomach.

ST. ANTONY OF EGYPT

Just as fish die if they stay too long out of water, so monks who loiter outside their cells or pass their time with men of the world lose the intensity of inner peace.

ST. ANTONY OF EGYPT

If a king wanted to take possession of his enemy's city, he would begin by cutting off the water and the food, and so his enemies, dying of hunger, would submit to him. It is the same with the passions of the flesh: if a man goes about fasting and hungry, the enemies of his soul grow weak.

ST. JOHN THE DWARF

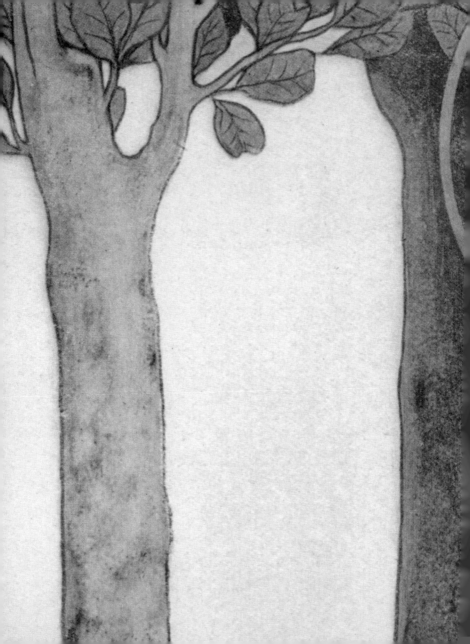

chapter 4
Myths and Realities

Legendary Lives

The lives and deaths of some early saints are recorded in reliable historical documents, but the biographies of many others have been buried in later tales that mix myth and fact. The most influential collection of such stories was the *Legenda Aurea* (The Golden Legend), which was put together in about 1260 by Jacobus de Voragine, Archbishop of Genoa. It became one of the most widely copied and translated texts in Europe, and was one of the first books to be printed.

Medieval biographies like these were not history as we now understand it; their authors thought that the moral purpose of a story was more important than its literal truth. The most extreme result of this approach was that stories were written about saints that had never existed, and some of these became the most popular stories of all. The legends of SS. Barbara and Margaret of Antioch won them enormous followings in the Middle Ages, but we now doubt whether either ever lived. Margaret's legend had been declared of doubtful authenticity by Pope Gelasius in 494, but her story—in which she endures spectacular sufferings, including being swallowed by a dragon—proved irrepressible. In England alone, more than 200 churches were dedicated to her. Hers was one of the voices heard by Joan of Arc. There was a statue of her in Joan's parish church at Domrémy. That statue is still there today.

previous page: **St. Brigid, Frederick Cayley Robinson, 1862–1927, English**
The real story of St. Brigid is buried under delightful myths.
right: **St. Margaret, Nicolas Poussin, 1594–1665, French**
Margaret kneels upon the dragon that swallowed her.

Facts and Fictions

St. Barbara's life story is as dramatic as St. Margaret's. At its climax, she is beheaded by her own father, who is struck dead by lightning—which is probably why prayers were said to her for protection against sudden death, which meant no chance for sacramental absolution and the risk of eternal damnation. Such prayers must have been frequent in an age when plague, war or famine might occur at any time.

Saints' stories such as those of Margaret and Barbara may not be good history, but they are certainly good stories. Identifying their origin is next to impossible. Some were probably first told as fiction, and were then passed on by later listeners as fact. The legend of the *Seven Sleepers of Ephesus* tells of persecuted Christians who are walled up in a cave for their faith, and found alive 208 years later. This is obviously a pious variant of the folk tale *Rip Van Winkle*, but for centuries it was believed to be literally true. So was the story of St. Julian the Hospitaller, which is a fairy-tale parable of mistaken murder followed by penitence.

In a legend called Pelagia of Antioch, a beautiful, wealthy, and dissolute actress converts to Christianity, drops out of society, and lives the rest of her life as a hermit, dressed as a man. Her true identity and sex are only discovered after her death. There is no historical evidence for the story, but it gripped popular imagination. The germ of truth from which it grew might lie in one of St. John Chrysostom's homilies in which he mentions an actress from Antioch who became a nun.

Left: **St. Barbara, Michele Tosini, 1503–577, Italian**
In St. Barbara's legend, her father locks her in a tower, an iconic symbol that traditionally identifies her in paintings.

St. Veronica

The origins of St. Veronica are traditional rather than historical. A cloth bearing an image of the face of Jesus had been venerated in Rome since the eighth century—it was believed to be the veil used by a woman to wipe his face as he carried his cross. No such event happens in the gospels; the story is first told three or four centuries later. The name "Veronica" is given to that woman later still: it derives from the words *vera icon* meaning "true image." The story has long been recognized as a pious tradition: Archbishop (later St.) Carlo Borromeo deleted references to her from the liturgical books in Milan in the sixteenth century. Even so, many Catholic churches carry her name on their walls today. "Veronica wipes the face of Jesus" is one of the Stations of the Cross, a series of images that remind the faithful of the sufferings Christ endured on the way to Calvary. The pity felt by onlookers is remembered in the invented name of one of their number.

Huge numbers of unnamed saints were invented by exaggerating the scale of multiple martyrdoms. The tradition that St. Maurice was an officer of the Theban Legion who was put to death for refusing to sacrifice to the gods before a battle is thought to be reliable. The story that all the other men in that legion were executed at the same time for the same offense is not. The fifth-century Bishop Eucherius claimed 6,666 deaths, and later writers accepted the figure without question.

right: **Saint Veronica, Church of Notre Dame d'Ecouis, 14th century, French**
The story of this unhistorical saint continues to inspire devotion to the suffering Christ.

Ste PHILOMÈNE.

St. Philomena

The cult of the early Roman martyr St. Philomena is unusual because it began in modern times. We know exactly where, when, and why it started, and the case shows how easy it is for a legend to come to life. In 1802, a tomb containing the remains of a teenage girl was discovered in the Roman catacombs. The tomb was set behind three tiles. The writing on them made no sense until they were rearranged to read *PAX TECUM FILUMENA* ("Peace be with you, Philomena.") The relics were moved to the church of Mugnano, near Naples. A nun praying before a statue of Philomena claimed to have had a vision of the saint in which she recounted the details of her life.

Stories of miracles began to circulate. The Curé d'Ars (later St. Jean Vianney) became an admirer, and his reputation for holiness helped to popularize hers. The cult was officially approved in 1835 and Philomena was given a feast day, August 10th. Later scholars pointed out that the deliberate rearrangement of the tiles was a sign that the tomb had been reused, and that the bones were therefore not those of someone called Filumena. In any case, there was no evidence that either the person buried or Filumena herself had been a martyr or a saint. The cult was suppressed in 1961, but St. Philomena still has loyal followers. The saint that answers their prayers might perhaps have been a Roman martyr, but if so, we know nothing about her—not even her name.

left: **St. Philomena, lithograph, unnamed artist, 19th century**
St. Philomena's cult started with the mistaken identification of a tomb which was excavated in 1802.

Real Saints, Fictional Lives

Some of the most popular early saints were characters that had really existed, but about whom almost no historical facts were known. That did not stop detailed and colorful lives being written about them. Medieval historians believed that a good biography needed to include numerous anecdotes that showed the subject's character. If reliable anecdotes weren't available, unreliable ones were included, or fanciful ones made up. Such stories were readily believed by an audience that craved information about saints just as modern fans hunger for celebrity gossip.

All that can be said for certain about St. Cecilia is that she was a third-century Roman martyr. She is commemorated in the ancient eucharistic prayer that is still part of the Roman Catholic mass. The colorful legend that popularized her dates from the late fifth century. The version in *The Golden Legend* is retold in *The Second Nun's Tale* in Chaucer's *Canterbury Tales*, which was written about 1400. In it, Cecilia is married to a pagan, but has already consecrated herself to God. At her wedding, "whyl the organs maden melodye," she sang a different song in her heart, promising to preserve her virginity. That detail is the origin of her patronage of music.

**Near gilded organ-pipes, her hair
Wound with white roses, slept St. Cecily.**

ALFRED, LORD TENNYSON, *THE PALACE OF ART*

right: **St. Cecilia Playing the Organ, Jacques Stella, 1596–1657, French**
Nothing suggests that the historical St. Cecilia had any interest in music.

St. Lawrence

St. Lawrence was a Roman deacon who was martyred under Valerian in 258. Five ancient Roman basilicas were dedicated to him. He, too, is commemorated in the canon of the mass, and he is also recorded in the ancient martyrology, the *Depositio Martyrum*. Much else reported about him is traditional. The best known (but probably mistaken) story is that while he was roasting to death on a gridiron, he asked his executioners to turn him over because one side was cooked.

Even more remarkable stories characterize the fictional lives of two other real saints, Cosmas and Damian. Nothing is known about them except that they were martyred at Cyrrhus in Syria. Their legend turns them into twin brothers who were both doctors who offered their services for free—and those services included miraculous cures. The most famous of these is what we would today call a leg transplant. The story of that event makes the miracle more visually dramatic by making the donor a black man and the recipient white.

Quench in us, we beseech thee, O Lord, the flame of vice, even as Thou didst enable blessed Lawrence to overcome the fire of his sufferings.

ROMAN MISSAL

left: **The Martyrdom of St. Lawrence, 14th-century manuscript reproduced in *Les Arts Somptuaires,* French**

Lawrence was martyred in the persecutions of Valerian.

St. Sebastian

Another popular figure is St. Sebastian, a Roman martyr who suffered under Diocletian in about 300. His name, too, is recorded in the *Depositio Martyrum*, but all the other stories about him date from the fifth century. According to his legend, he is a captain of the Praetorian Guard who is sentenced to be shot to death with arrows for his faith. He miraculously survives, and is beaten to death. Seventh- and eighth-century pictures show him as an elderly man with a beard, but Renaissance artists turned him into a beautiful youth. There is no evidence that the real Sebastian was either.

I have a favorite saint ... It is Saint Sebastian, that youth at the stake, who, pierced by swords and arrows from all sides, smiles amidst his agony. Grace in suffering: that is the heroism symbolized by St. Sebastian.

THOMAS MANN

right: **Saint Sebastian, Jacometto Veneziano (1472–94), Italian**
The tradition of representing St. Sebastian as a beautiful youth has led to his becoming a homosexual icon.

SS. Christopher and Faith

All that is known for certain about St. Christopher is that he was a martyr who had a church dedicated to him in Bithynia in 452. The legend that emerged three centuries later describes him as a giant, called Offero, who was instructed in the faith by a hermit, and then served his fellow men by ferrying travelers across a river on his back. One of his passengers was the infant Jesus, who was almost impossible to carry because he bore the sins of the world on his shoulders. From that moment he was known as Christopher, meaning "Christ bearer" in Latin and Greek. Inspired by his miraculous encounter, Christopher went to preach the gospel in Lycia, where he was martyred under the emperor Decius. The story made him an ideal choice as a patron of travelers, and encouraged his cult to spread.

Devotion to the third-century martyr St. Faith (or St. Foy) was common throughout Christendom. This was not just because of the fanciful story of her life, but also by the presence of her relics at Conques, which is on the main pilgrim route to Compostela in Spain. The saint's remains are reputedly housed in an exquisite tenth-century jeweled reliquary that is memorable in its own right. It is still in the church's treasury today. According to the reliable *Martyrology of St. Jerome*, Faith was put to death in Agen. It does not say how she died; her legend has her roasted on a brass bed before being beheaded.

left: **St. Christopher and the Christ Child, Lucas Cranach the Elder, 1472–1553, German**
St. Christopher has always been patron saint of travelers, and in modern times he has become the protector of motorists in particular.

… another Julian there was that slew his father and mother by ignorance. and this man was noble and young, and gladly went for to hunt. and one time among all other he found an hart which returned toward him, and said to him, thou huntest me that shall slay thy father and mother…

GOLDEN LEGEND: *JULIAN THE HOSPITALLER*

… it is in doubt of that which is said that they slept three hundred and sixty-two years, for they were raised the year of our lord four hundred and seventy-eight, and Decius reigned but one year and three months, and that was in the year of our lord two hundred and seventy, and so they slept but two hundred and eight years.

GOLDEN LEGEND: *THE SEVEN SLEEPERS OF EPHESUS*

… and then appeared a horrible dragon and assailed her, and would have devoured her, but she made the sign of the cross, and anon he vanished away. and in another place it is said that he swallowed her into his belly, she making the sign of the cross. and the belly brake asunder, and so she issued out all whole and sound. this swallowing and breaking of the belly of the dragon is said that it is apocryphal.

GOLDEN LEGEND: *MARGARET OF ANTIOCH*

but when her father descended from the mountain, a fire from heaven descended on him, and consumed him in such wise that there could not be found only ashes of all his body.

GOLDEN LEGEND: *ST. BARBARA*

… and when the sick man awoke and felt no pain, he put forth his hand and felt his leg without hurt, and then took a candle, and saw well that it was not his thigh, but that it was another.

GOLDEN LEGEND: *SS. COSMO AND DAMIAN*

George, Saint and Hero

St. George is believed to have been martyred in 303, but nothing more is known of him than this, though we do know that churches were dedicated to him in the sixth century in Jerusalem and Antioch. He is also mentioned in the decree *De libris recipiendis* attributed to Pope Gelasius, which is believed to have been published in about 495. Unfortunately, that reference simply shows how impossible it was to identify the historical St. George even then: "George must be classed with that category of saints whose names are justly reverenced among men, but whose acts on earth are known only to God."

Despite this, George's popularity was boundless. In the East, he was given the title *Megalomartyros*—the Great Martyr. By the beginning of the sixth century—possibly earlier—his tomb at Lydda in Palestine was a place of pilgrimage, and many miraculous cures were associated with it. An early legend describes him as a soldier who refuses the emperor Diocletian's order to sacrifice to the gods. He is imprisoned and tortured over a seven-year period, during which time he is three times killed and three times brought back to life. But that fiction has long been overshadowed by the St. George in shining armor who slew a dragon, a tale that was already popular before a definitive version appeared in the thirteenth century in *The Golden Legend*.

This St. George was a knight born in Cappadocia, whose travels took him to Silene in Libya. The city was terrorized by a dragon, which the people placated by feeding it two sheep a day. When the sheep had all been eaten, the king ordered that the dragon should be given a human being, chosen by lottery. Finally, the hand of fate fell on his daughter, and St. George found her waiting for her doom. When the dragon appeared, he made the sign of the cross over it with his sword, then brought it down with a spear. He led the injured creature back to the city, using the maid's girdle as a leash. The people were terrified, but George told them that they had nothing to fear: if they accepted baptism, he would slay the dragon. They agreed, he struck off the creature's head, and "then were there well fifteen thousand men baptized, without women and children, and the king did do make a church there of our Lady and of St. George, in the which yet soundeth a fountain of living water, which healeth sick people that drink thereof."

The story ends with George's martyrdom during the Diocletian and Maximian persecutions. The dating is probably accurate, but the details are made up. George is so badly tortured that his entrails burst out, and they are sprinkled with salt. He is plunged into a cauldron of molten lead, but "by the virtue of our Lord it seemed that he was in a bath well at ease." He is then beheaded. By the time Caxton's anglicized *The Golden Legend* was published, George was well established as the "patron of this realm of England and the cry of men of war."

**I see you stand like greyhounds in the slips,
Straining upon the start. The game's afoot:
Follow your spirit; and, upon this charge
Cry God for Harry, England and St. George!**

SHAKESPEARE, *HENRY V*

next page: **St. George and the Dragon, Paolo Uccello, 1397–1475, Italian**
St. George is the definitive knight in shining armor.

Saints and Dragons

Dragons feature in the stories of at least 30 saints. In *The Golden Legend*, SS. George, Margaret of Antioch and Donatus slay dragons, and another is killed by the men transporting the body of St. James the Greater. St. Martha paralyzes one so that others can kill it. St. Simeon Stylites tames one, St. Silvester disables one and St. Matthew subdues two. St. Philip commands his to go off into the desert and never return. The dragons in all those legends are represented as real. Silvester's dragon lives at the bottom of a pit. Philip's "right great dragon" appears from under a pagan idol and kills three men before he drives it away. Matthew's' fearsome pair "cast fire and sulphur by their mouths and nostrils."

To the people of the Middle Ages, the dragon was a real, living creature. They had not seen one in the flesh, but they knew what dragons looked like because they had seen representations of them in the wall paintings and stained glass of their churches. They had heard (and their clergy had read) descriptions of them in the lives of the saints. Martha's "great dragon" in *The Golden Legend* is "half beast and half fish, greater than an ox, longer than a horse, having teeth sharp as a sword, and horned on either side, head like a lion, tale like a serpent, and defended … with two wings either side". Human strength alone could not possibly subdue such a creature.

The dragon was also a symbol of evil that everybody recognized. It is the devil incarnate. The Apocalypse of St. John (20: 2) describes a vision of "the dragon, the old serpent, which is the Devil and Satan." In the legend of St. Michael the Archangel, the saint drives "the dragon Lucifer and all his followers" from Heaven. Standards bearing a dragon with a long cloth tail were carried in Rogationtide processions in which evil spirits were driven out of the parish. The ceremonies ended with the removal of the tail as a sign that the power of the Devil had been overcome. The same symbolism is found in the legends of the saints. The dragon stories are allegorical representations of the defeat of error by truth, of evil by good, and of paganism by the teachings of the gospel. The dragons are not overcome by physical, but by spiritual power. The sign of the cross is enough to break a dragon in half in the legend of St. James the Greater, to cause two to fall asleep at the feet of St. Matthew, to bring down the monster later slain by St. George, and, in one version of the legend of St. Margaret of Antioch, to cause the dragon that has swallowed her to burst asunder.

People in the Middle Ages understood the allegorical significance of these tales, but they also believed them to be literally true. The life of St. Silvester in *The Golden Legend* makes the point explicitly: "Thus was the city of Rome delivered from double death, that was from the culture and worshipping of false idols, and from the venom of the dragon." The frequent appearance of dragons is one of many indications that the legends of the saints are not to be judged as history, but as expressions of poetic and moral truth.

Great Saint George, our patron, help us,
In the conflict be thou nigh;
Help us in that daily battle,
Where each one must win or die!

J.W. REEKS

The holy Georcus was in
heathenish days a rich ealderman,
under the fierce Caesar Dacianus
in the shire of Cappadocia ...

AELFRIC, *LIFE OF ST. GEORGE*

In sum, it seems likely that the story of
Veronica is a delightful legend without
any historical basis; that Veronica is a
purely fictitious, not a historical character;
and that the story was invented to
explain the relic.

DAVID HUGH FARMER, *THE OXFORD DICTIONARY OF SAINTS* FIFTH EDITION, 2003

Every one loved St. Bridget. Even the sunbeams liked to be near her. One day an April shower came on, and, as she entered her cell, she flung her wet cloak over a sunbeam shining through the window, thinking it was a wooden beam. The bright ray willingly held up the mantle hour after hour, but at last the sun set, and the sunbeam was anxious to be gone too. So it begged that Bridget would come and take her cloak.

F.H. LEE, *THE CHILDREN'S BOOK OF SAINTS,* 1940

I saw a shining bird at the window, and it sat on the altar. I was unable to look at it because of the rays that surrounded it, like those of the sun … "And who are you?" said St. Brendan. "The angel Michael," it said, "come to speak with you … to bless you and to make music for you from your Lord."

IRISH, TENTH-CENTURY, AUTHOR UNKNOWN

The Legend of St. Catherine

St. Catherine of Alexandria was one of the most popular saints of the Middle Ages, but it is impossible to identify a real person upon whom her quite extraordinary legend was built. She was believed to be a fourth-century martyr, but the first recorded reference to her is not found until half a millennium later, when her remains were said to have been carried to Mount Sinai by angels. That 500-year interval is enough in itself to make her historical existence doubtful. A life of such dramatic sanctity would surely have been recorded somewhere in literature or art. It may be that the remains venerated at the monastery on Mount Sinai are indeed those of a saint called Catherine. It may be that they were carried there by angelic monks. What can be said for sure, though, is that the life later written for St. Catherine is a work of pure fiction that conforms to a classic literary type. It is one of the "virgin-martyr" legends that are among the best loved tales of the saints.

Thou art St. Catherine, and invisible angels
Bear thee across these chasms and precipices,
Lest thou shouldst dash thy feet against a stone!

HENRY WADSWORTH LONGFELLOW, *CHRISTUS: A MYSTERY*

right: **Catherine of Alexandria, Egyptian saint and martyr, showing St. Agnes the instruments of her torture, from Paul Lacroix,** *Le Moyen Âge et La Renaissance***, 19th century, French**
St. Catherine's instrument of torture makes her patron saint of wheelwrights.

The version of Catherine's life in *The Golden Legend* is full of colorful detail and incident, and is 9,500 words long, which is double the length of the life of St. Peter, and more than three times that of St. Augustine of Canterbury. It claims to be based on the life of Catherine written by St. Athanasius, and describes her as a beautiful young Queen of Cyprus, who is descended from the emperor Constantine. She refuses to marry unless the man is so perfect that he is born of a virgin. The Virgin Mary has Catherine brought miraculously to heaven, describing her as "a chosen vessel of special grace before all women who live." Catherine is baptized; Our Lady is her godmother, and then:

Our Lord espoused her in joining himself to her by spiritual marriage, promising ever to keep her in all her life in this world, and after this life to reign perpetually in his bliss.

THE GOLDEN LEGEND

If any of that were true, it would be enough to make Catherine the greatest of the saints, occupying a position second only to Mary herself. But there is even more. Catherine returns to earth and rebukes the emperor Maxentius for his worship of false gods. He sends for fifty philosophers to persuade her to reject Christianity; she wins them over, and they are executed for their new-found faith. The emperor's own wife is converted, and she is martyred, too. Maxentius orders Catherine to be "despoiled naked and beaten with scorpions," but she remains steadfast in her faith. He offers to make her his empress, but she rejects him. Furious, he orders her tortured on "four wheels of iron, environed with sharp razors" that are then brought together to crush her to death. But an angel smashes the wheels, and 4,000 onlookers are killed by the flying parts, an incident commemorated in the name of the "Catherine wheel" firework. When she is beheaded, milk, not blood, runs from her severed head. It is an undeniably wonderful story, but it is certainly not history. In 1969, the Vatican removed Catherine from the calendar of saints, but her cult proved extraordinarily persistent, and her feast was restored for local use in 2001. There is, after all, no more proof that she didn't exist than that she did.

To recognize that many of the stories told of the saints are flights of pious fancy need not lead to cynicism. The Belgian hagiographer Hippolyte Delehaye (1859–1941) wrote that when he read *The Golden Legend*, it was "difficult at times to refrain from a smile." But it was "a sympathetic and tolerant smile," because "the saints practice all the virtues in a superhuman degree: gentleness, mercy, the forgiveness of injuries, mortification, renunciation; and they render these virtues lovable, and they urge Christians to practice them. Their life is, in truth, the concrete realization of the spirit of the Gospel, and from the very fact that it brings home to us this sublime ideal, legend, like all poetry, can claim a higher degree of truth than history itself."

Saintly Thrillers

Violence and sex are classic ingredients in storytelling, and both are found in the legends of the saints. The sufferings that many early martyrs endured were terrible enough, but the torments later writers invented for them were even worse. The only historical certainty about the martyrdom of St. Erasmus is that it happened in about 300, but medieval legends supply more than fifty tortures to accompany it. These include rolling him in pitch and setting him alight, scourging him with brambles, boiling him in oil, and winding out his entrails with a windlass. The *Passion of Clement and Agathangelus* describes how, over twenty-eight years, these two saints are flayed alive, torn with hooks, beaten with rods, burned with torches, buried in quicklime, flung to wild beasts, and tied to a white-hot bed frame that it is then thrown into a furnace.

Such details were invented to inspire admiration for the heroism of the martyrs, but they also provide excitement. The thrill is not just spiritual. It is even less pure when cruelty is combined with sex, as it is in the legends of the early virgin-martyrs. The *Lives* of the real saints Agatha and Agnes, the doubtful Margaret and Barbara, and the myth-surrounded Catherine of Alexandria are essentially reworkings of the same story. Beautiful young Christian women consecrate themselves to virginity, and reject the lustful advances of powerful pagan men. They are tortured in sexually sadistic ways before they are killed.

right: **Martyrdom of St. Agatha, Giovanni Battista Tiepolo, 1696–1770, Italian**
St Agatha certainly suffered martyrdom, but the tortures described in her legend were made up.

Thirteen-year-old St. Agnes is stripped and cast into a brothel. St. Lucy is saved from a similar fate by a miracle. Barbara is stripped and flogged, strung up between two trees, beaten with staves, burned with firebrands, and has her breasts cut off. According to *The Golden Legend*, Agatha's "breasts and mammels" are cut off, too, but only after they have been "tormented" and "drawn." In the legend of Catherine of Alexandria, it is not the main heroine, but the wife of the wicked emperor whose "paps" are torn off "with tongs of iron." Margaret keeps her breasts, but is beaten with rods, tortured with fire and water and has her flesh—her physical beauty—ripped from her with iron combs.

Such legends certainly popularised their heroines, but they also provided salacious entertainment. The fictional lives of the virgin-martyrs were turned into plays that were performed all over Europe. A life of Saint Catherine of Alexandria was widely performed between the twelfth and sixteenth centuries in England. The play of St. Barbara was a regular sellout in sixteenth-century France. The *Rappresentazione di Sancta Christina* ran through fifteen editions in 1490's Florence. Stage directions require the saint's breasts to be torn with billhooks.

The cruelties of the virgin-martyr legends suggest a fear of female sexuality. The tortures invented for male martyrs do not focus on sex. But these legends in this group also celebrate virginity in a positive way. Celibate monks and nuns looked to the virgin-martyrs as heroic role models. Lay men and women prayed to them for help because they believed that the combination of martyrdom and virginity made them doubly powerful advocates at the court of Heaven. Their stories have a double power, too—the life of a virgin-martyr cannot be told without at least some reference to sex and to violence. The authors of the medieval legends found a way of providing plenty of both.

Celtic Saints

The Celtic church was founded by missionaries from Rome and Gaul in the second and third centuries, then driven to the margins of the British Isles by the Saxon invasions of the late fifth century. It survived in Ireland, Scotland, Wales, and Cornwall, where it developed independent traditions of its own. One of these was to bestow the title "saint" freely, so there is a disproportionately large number of Celtic saints. Few of their lives were recorded by their contemporaries, and by the time they were written down, facts were mostly buried under legend.

One of the most popular Celtic saints even today is St. Brigid of Ireland (St. Bride), who is believed to have died in about 525. Later *Lives* describe her as the founder of the monastery of Kildare, but nearly everything else written about her is myth mixed with folklore. Her claimed miracles include hanging her cloak upon a sunbeam, turning stone into salt, and changing bathwater into beer.

The fifth-century St. Patrick is the subject of many legends, including the claim that he expelled all the snakes from Ireland, which is an obvious allegory for driving religious error from the whole country. What is known of him for certain is found in his autobiographical *Confessio* and his *Letter to Coroticus*, in which he condemns the contemporary trade in slaves. The son of a Romano-British civil servant, he had himself been captured by pirates and held as a slave for six years in Ireland, the country he was later sent to evangelize.

We know less about the sixth-century Welsh abbot St. Beuno—his life was written 800 years later. His cult was so well established that his shrine was being visited long after such practices were forbidden after the Reformation. His legend claims that he restored to life his niece, St. Winifrede whose shrine at Holywell is still visited by pilgrims today.

The life of the great Celtic holy man, St. Columba (c. 521–97) is recorded in a biography written a century after his death by St. Adomnan, abbot of Iona, the monastery that Columba founded on a Scottish island. It describes a life of miracles and prophecies, but perhaps Columba's greatest miracle was to establish a center of learning that was so famous that monks visited it from every part of the world.

St. Aidan (d. 651) also founded a scholarly community. He was the first bishop and abbot of the Holy Island of Lindisfarne, which produced the Lindisfarne Gospels, a masterpiece of calligraphy that fuses Roman, Coptic, and Eastern artistic elements with Anglo-Saxon and Celtic traditions. What little we know of St. Caedmon (d. 680) is found in the writings of St. Bede, who describes how the herdsman was given the gift of song and poetry in a dream. Bede quotes a fragment of his verse, but everything else that he wrote has been lost.

Another Celtic saint about whom there are more legends than facts is St. Brendan (c. 486–575), who traveled so widely that he is known as Brendan the Navigator. His fame was spread not by his real achievements, which include the foundation of several Irish abbeys, but by a romance that was written centuries after his death. The Navigation of St. Brendan describes a fantastic journey to a promised land across the Atlantic Ocean, in which the saint's adventures include riding on the back of a whale, and meeting Judas Iscariot on an iceberg, on day release from hell, in return for the one act of kindness that he had performed during his life.

Saint Brandan sails the northern main;
The brotherhoods of saints are glad.
He greets them once, he sails again.
So late!—such storms!—The Saint is mad!

He heard across the howling seas
Chime convent bells on wintry nights,
He saw on spray-swept Hebrides
Twinkle the monastery lights;

But north, still north, Saint Brandan steer'd;
And now no bells, no convents more!
The hurtling Polar lights are near'd,
The sea without a human shore.

MATTHEW ARNOLD, *SAINT BRANDAN*

chapter 5
Relics and Pilgrimages

The Relics of Saints

The tradition of honoring saints' physical remains began early in the history of the Church. An eyewitness account of events that occurred in 155 tells how the Christian community gathered up St. Polycarp's bones, described as "more valuable than precious stones and finer than refined gold." The Christians then "laid them in a suitable place" where they could gather "to celebrate the birthday of his martyrdom." The tombs of the martyrs had become meeting-places, where Christians celebrated the Eucharist and honored the memory of their saints.

By the time that the Edict of Milan ended religious persecution in the Roman Empire in 313, the tradition of celebrating the Eucharist in the presence of a saint's remains was firmly established. When the underground church surfaced, it brought its relics with it, sometimes literally: martyrs' remains were taken from tombs and moved to newly built churches or were carried from place to place to inspire the faithful.

That inspiration was all the greater when miraculous cures associated with those relics were reported, as had happened since New Testament times. "Now God worked unusual miracles by the hands of Paul, so that even handkerchiefs ... were brought from his body to the sick, and the diseases left them ...." (Acts19:11–12).

previous page: **The annual procession of the Holy Blood in Bruges from a book of Belgian folklore**
A great parade honors the relic brought to Belgium in 1150.
right: **Monks carry home relics from the Levant, 10th-century Flemish manuscript reproduced in *Les Arts Somptuaires*, 1857–8**
Relics were needed to consecrate new churches.

MVLTI CVRANTVR CVM CORPORA SCA LEVANTVR

The Power of Relics

In *The City of God* St. Augustine of Hippo (354–430) records the miracle that occurred when the remains of St. Stephen were brought to North Africa in 416: "A blind woman entreated that she might be led to the bishop who was carrying the relics. He gave her the flowers he was carrying. She took them, applied them to her eyes, and forthwith saw."

In the West, disturbing saints' bones was considered disrespectful, and the custom was for the church to be brought to the martyr, not the martyr to the church. There, the need for relics was largely met by creating "secondary" relics by touching pieces of cloth to the remains in saints' tombs. But "primary" relics—the bodies themselves—were still keenly sought after, and traffic in them continued and grew. The supply was increased by "partition," the division of the remains into parts.

Interest in non-bodily relics was spurred by the discovery of remains believed to be those of Christ's cross in 335 while digging foundations for the Holy Sepulchre in Jerusalem. A generation later, St. Cyril of Jerusalem wrote that fragments of the cross had been distributed all over the world. In 787, the Council of Nicaea made the use of relics to consecrate new churches a requirement of canon law. As northern Europe was converted to Christianity, more churches were built, and more relics were needed to consecrate them. Churches, cathedrals, and abbeys competed for the most prestigious. The Emperor Charlemagne (742–814) built a cathedral for his capital at Aachen, and used his wealth and influence to amass a spectacular collection.

left: **Reliquary in the form of a bust of Charlemagne, 1349, German**
Relics collected by Charlemagne are still displayed today.

The Great Collections

Many relics were brought from the Holy Land to Europe during the Crusades, including relics of Christ's Passion, which inspired the faithful to think of their suffering Savior with pity and gratitude. King Louis IX of France (1214–70), later declared a saint, obtained what was thought to be Christ's crown of thorns from Baldwin II, emperor of Constantinople, . He built the Sainte Chapelle in Paris to house it. Frederick the Wise of Saxony (1463–1525) had a treasury containing more than 18,000 relics in the Castle Church at Wittenburg. The collection included 200 bone fragments of the Holy Innocents, thirty-three pieces of the True Cross, and a branch from Moses' Burning Bush. Charlemagne's great collection included pieces of cloth believed to be the cloak of the Blessed Virgin, the cloth that wrapped the head of John the Baptist, the swaddling cloth of the Infant Jesus, and the loin cloth worn by Christ on the cross. Still there, they are exposed for veneration every seven years.

I bequeath to my beloved wife, Lady of Arundel and Maltravers, a cross containing a large piece of the Holy Cross. This is now in pledge; when it is recovered, each of my children is to have a piece ... but my wife is to have the larger piece for her life. Afterward the cross and the larger piece of the Holy Cross to go to the church of Stokecours, forever.

FROM THE WILL OF RICHARD POYNINGS, KNIGHT, PROVED 31ST OCTOBER 1430

right: **St. Louis bringing the relics of Jesus' passion to Paris, reproduction of a stained-glass window in La Sainte Chapelle, 19th-century, French** Louis IX of France was both a saint and a king.

Real or Fake?

It is at least possible that some relics were genuine. Scientific tests on the veil of the Virgin Mary venerated at Chartres place its origin in first-century Palestine. The authenticity of the Turin Shroud, the winding sheet that appears to bear the imprint of the body of Christ, continues to cause debate. But many other relics have long been recognized as fictional to the point of absurdity. The church of Santa Maria Maggiore in Rome and the Chapel Royal at Windsor displayed vessels containing the breast milk of the Virgin, and the abbeys of Hailes and Westminster owned "crystals" containing Christ's blood.

Nobody could claim to own a relic of Jesus' resurrected body, but objects claimed to be his milk teeth and umbilical cord were displayed. So, too, was his circumcized foreskin, venerated at the Rome church of St. John Lateran. Other "Holy Foreskins" were on show in France, Germany, the Netherlands, and Spain. St. Apollonia was the patron saint of dentistry; her teeth had been knocked out before she was martyred in Alexandria in about 249. At a time when health was poor and surgery painful, prayers to her were frequent and urgent. It is possible that some saints' teeth in circulation were genuine; what is certain is that they cannot *all* have been. Nor could all three heads displayed in churches at Constantinople, Angers, and Amiens have belonged to John the Baptist.

previous page: **Procession of the Relic of the True Cross in St. Mark's Square, Venice, Gentile Bellini, 1429–1507, Italian**
The painting commemorates a miraculous cure in 1444.
right: **Part of the first photograph of the Turin Shroud, 1898**
Scientists continue to debate the authenticity of this inspiring relic.

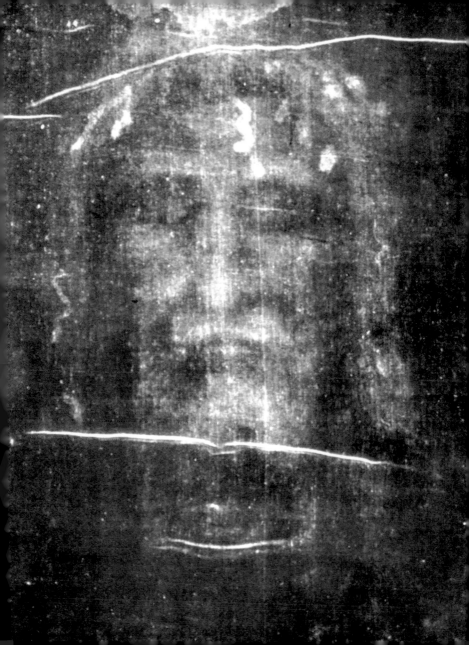

Trading in Relics

Relics became a valuable commodity, and pedlars selling forgeries and fakes traveled the fairs of medieval Europe. The Franciscan preacher Saint Bernardino of Siena (1380–1444) said that there was more milk of the Virgin in circulation than all the buffalo cows of Lombardy could have produced. The Pardoner in Chaucer's *Canterbury Tales* boasts that he earns a hundred marks a year selling worthless rags and bones that he passes off as relics with miraculous properties. "Then I display my hollow crystal stones crammed full of rags and bones—relics they are, so everyone thinks!" The character is fictional, but fifteenth-century readers would have recognized the type. It certainly wasn't new—St. Augustine (354–430) had described rogues dressed as monks selling false relics a thousand years earlier. The cult of relics had contained the potential for corruption from the start.

Thanne shewe I forth my longe cristal stones,
Ycrammed ful of cloutes and of bones;
Relikes been they, as wenen they echoon.

GEOFFREY CHAUCER, *PROLOGUE TO THE PARDONER'S TALE*

left: **The Pardoner, detail from the "The Ellesmere Chaucer,"**
c. 1400–1405, English
Chaucer makes the Pardoner the most contemptible of his pilgrims.
next page: **An Auction of Relics at Avignon, Thomas Rowlandson, 1756–1827, English**
The renowned English cartoonist brilliantly satirizes the trade in relics.

The Role of Relics

The veneration of relics has always contained the potential for good. The instinct to preserve mementoes of loved ones is universal, and the early Christians' reverence for the bones of their martyrs fostered a loving familiarity with the saints themselves. The presence of their relics encouraged people to picture them not as distant heroes, but as friends and fellow members of the extended Christian family. The Dominican theologian St. Thomas Aquinas (c. 1225–74) set out the theological basis for this relationship in his *Summa Theologica*:

We should show honor to the saints of God, as being members of Christ, the children and friends of God, and our intercessors. Therefore, in memory of them we ought to honor any relics of theirs in a fitting manner.

That "fitting manner" had been defined centuries before by St. Jerome (c. 341–420) in his Letter to Riparius:

We do not worship, we do not adore, for fear that we should bow down to the creature rather than to the Creator, but we venerate the relics of the martyrs in order the better to adore Him whose martyrs they are.

Unfortunately, the line between piety and superstition was easily crossed. In the Middle Ages, the abbey at Bath possessed a chain said to have bound St. Peter; pregnant women wound it about themselves to encourage a safe delivery. The same protection was sought at Westminster from the girdle of Our Lady, and at Bruton from the belt of St. Mary Magdalene. Other relics were believed to be particularly powerful against conditions and ailments ranging from headaches and fevers to lost cattle. Complaints against obvious abuses were followed by doubts about the value of relics at all. The Dutch humanist scholar Desiderius Erasmus (1466–1536) wrote:

We kiss the shoes of the saints and their dirty kerchiefs, while we leave their writings, their holiest and truest relics, to lie unread.

Today, relics figure far less prominently in the imagination of most Christians, and the church no longer draws attention to the more doubtful treasures it has accumulated over time. However, the most ancient and uncorrupted tradition associated with the relics of martyrs and other saints continues. The altars upon which mass is celebrated are still required to enclose saints' relics by canon law.

Saints Preserved

One sign that has traditionally been taken to indicate that a person was a saint is the fact that his or her body has not suffered corruption after death. This may be discovered by chance, when a saint's body is moved to a new church or shrine or, sometimes, the body is exhumed to see if corruption has taken place. The body of the Lourdes visionary St. Bernadette Soubirous (1844–79) was examined in 1909, 1919, and 1925, and on each occasion was found to be substantially incorrupt. The first examination was conducted by two doctors, David and Jourdan. They wrote:

The coffin was opened in the presence of the Bishop of Nevers, the mayor of the town, his principal deputy, several canons, and ourselves … The face was dull white. The skin clung to the muscles and the muscles adhered to the bones. The sockets of the eyes were covered by the eye-lids … The nose was dilated and shrunken. The mouth was open slightly and it could be seen that the teeth were still in place. The hands, which were crossed on her breast, were perfectly preserved, as were the nails. The hands still held a rusting rosary. The veins on the forearms stood out.

The 1925 examination was conducted by Doctors Talon and Comte. Comte wrote: "The body of the Venerable Bernadette is intact, the skeleton is complete, the muscles have atrophied, but are well preserved; only the skin, which has shriveled, seems to have suffered from the effects of the damp in the coffin. It has taken on a greyish tinge and is covered with patches of mildew and quite a large number of crystals and calcium salts; but the body does not seem to have putrefied, nor has any decomposition of the cadaver set in, although this would be expected and normal after such a long period in a vault hollowed out of the earth."

A thin wax mask was made for the saint's face and hands, to cover the blackening of the skin and conceal the shrunken nose and eyes. Since her beatification in 1925, Bernadette's body has been displayed in a glass case in the convent in Nevers.

The body of the Curé d'Ars, St. Jean-Marie-Baptiste Vianney (1786–1859) was found to be incorrupt when it was exhumed in 1904. Today, it is displayed above the main altar in the Ars Basilica. The body of the visionary St. Catherine Labouré (1806–76) was discovered to be in a perfect state of preservation in 1933. It can now be seen in the Chapel of Our Lady of the Miraculous Medal in Paris.

Some saints' bodies that are described as incorrupt are in a less remarkable condition. The website of the Basilica of St. Rita of Cascia (1377–1447) announces that "her face, hands and feet are mummified" and that her skeleton is complete. When the tomb of the third-century Roman martyr St. Cecilia was opened in 1599, her body was found to be incorrupt, but shortly afterward, it turned to dust.

Now I look day by day
for that time when the cross of the Lord,
which once I saw in a dream here on earth,
will fetch me away from this fleeting life
and lift me to the home of joy and happiness
where the people of God are seated at the feast
in eternal bliss, and set me down
where I may live in glory unending and share
the glory of the saints.

THE DREAM OF THE ROOD, TRANSLATED FROM ANGLO-SAXON

We adore Thy cross, O Lord: and we praise and glorify Thy
holy Resurrection: for behold, by the wood of the cross,
joy has come into the whole world.

GOOD FRIDAY ANTIPHON, ROMAN MISSAL

Then glad in mind, resolute in zeal, he fell to digging in
the earth, under the turf, for the glorious tree, till he found
it, buried twenty feet down, hidden in darkness under the
steep cliff. There he came on three crosses together
concealed in the ground ...

CYNEWULF, *ELENE* TRANSLATED FROM ANGLO-SAXON

those who maintain that veneration and honor are not due to the relics of the saints, or that these and other memorials are honored by the faithful without profit, and that the places dedicated to the memory of the saints for the purpose of obtaining their aid are visited in vain, are to be utterly condemned ...

COUNCIL OF TRENT, 1563

... in the invocation of saints, the veneration of relics, and the sacred use of images, every superstition shall be removed, all filthy lucre be abolished ...That these things may be the more faithfully observed, the holy council decrees that ... no new miracles be accepted and no relics recognized unless they have been investigated and approved by the ... bishop...

COUNCIL OF TRENT, 1563

Pilgrimages

Pilgrimages to the Holy Land began in early times. The fourth-century historian Eusebius of Caesarea mentions a pilgrimage to Jerusalem by a Bishop Alexander in 217, and the Roman empress St. Helena (c. 250–330) made a pilgrimage to Palestine after her late-life conversion to Christianity. Tradition asserts that she found there the remains of the True Cross; reports of the discovery increased the flow of pilgrims. Others were inspired by St. Jerome (c. 341–420), who traveled to Jerusalem in 385. Among those who followed him were St. Paula (d. 404), a Roman aristocrat who founded convents and a guesthouse for pilgrims in Bethlehem. She wrote from there reporting that she had seen pilgrims from Gaul, Britain, Armenia, Persia, India, and Ethiopia.

As Christianity spread out across the world, distant Christian converts felt drawn to visit their spiritual roots, and pilgrimages were made to as well as from Rome. These increased when pilgrimages to the Holy Land became impossible after the Moslem Turks captured Jerusalem in 1071. The main purpose of the Roman pilgrimage was to visit the tomb of the apostles SS. Peter (d. c. 64) and Paul (d. c. 65). Several Roman pilgrimages are recorded in *The Ecclesiastical History of the English People* by the Venerable Bede (673–735), including journeys by the Northumbrian saints Benedict Biscop (628–89) and Wilfrid (c. 633–709).

left: 15th-century breviary, reproduced in the magazine *L'Illustration*, 1936, French
Helena, empress and saint, discovers the remains of the cross on which Jesus was crucified.

Santiago de Compostela

By the tenth century, a third world center of pilgrimage was established. Santiago de Compostela was believed to be the resting place of the bones of the apostle St. James the Greater (d. 44)—(Sant Iago is the Spanish form of St. James.) A seventh-century legend describes his missionary journey to Spain, but there is no contemporary evidence for it. The claim that his relics were returned there after his martyrdom was not made until the ninth century. His body was said to have been put in a rudderless boat, which angels guided to the Atlantic coast of northern Spain, where it was found and buried by a local queen. The tomb was rediscovered eight centuries later and the relics were authenticated by the local bishop.

Devotion to St. James spread rapidly, and he became a focus of Christian resistance to the Moorish invaders of Spain. His help in conquering the Islamic invaders was acknowledged in his title *Matamoros,* "the Moor-slayer," and many pictures or statues show St. Iago as a warrior with a dead Moor at his feet. During the eleventh and twelfth centuries, more than a half a million pilgrims a year journeyed to Compostela from all over Christendom. Monasteries were established along the major routes, offering pilgrims spiritual and medical care as well as accommodation. Several, such as Vézelay, (which had a shrine of St. Mary Magdalene,) and Conques, (which had the relics of the virgin-martyr St. Faith) were centers of pilgrimage in their own right.

right: **St. James, popular print, Spanish**
St. James wears a pilgrim's shell and carries a pilgrim's staff with a water bottle attached to it.

Pilgrims' Badges

Medieval pilgrims wore metal badges that were emblems representing their place of pilgrimage. For those who had been to Jerusalem, this was two crossed palms. Several signs identified Rome: the crossed keys of St. Peter, the heads of SS. Peter and Paul, or the Vernicle, the cloth bearing the imprint of Christ's face that was displayed in the city. Pilgrims to St. Catherine's tomb on Mount Sinai wore a badge in the shape of her wheel. St. Iago's emblem was a scallop shell. The badge of the magnificent shrine of the Three Kings at Cologne was an emblem showing the Kings guided by a star to the newborn Jesus.

**Ye may see by my signs that are set in my hat
That I have walked full wide in wet and in dry
And sought good saints for my soul's health.**

WILLIAM LANGLAND, *THE VISION OF PIERS THE PLOWMAN (MODERNIZED)*

left: **The Scala Santa, Rome, F. Ferra, 1830s, Italian**
Pilgrims to Rome climb the Scala Santa (Holy Stair) on their knees. The steps are said to have been taken from the palace of Pontius Pilate in Jerusalem.

St. Thomas Becket

Pilgrims came from all social classes. Chaucer's *Canterbury Tales*, written about 1400, describes a fictional group that includes a lawyer, a miller, a monk, a merchant, a sailor, a knight, a physician, two nuns, and a housewife. Theirs is one of medieval England's most famous pilgrimages, to the shrine that housed the relics of St. Thomas Becket (1118–70) at Canterbury in Kent. Offerings left by countless pilgrims from England and further afield were used to decorate the shrine magnificently with jewels, gold, and silver.

And specially from every shire's end
Of England to Canterbury they wend
The holy blissful martyr for to seek

GEOFFREY CHAUCER, *CANTERBURY TALES*

Thomas was born in London to Norman parents. He was educated at Merton Abbey, Paris, Bologna, and Auxerre, and then ordained as a deacon. In 1154 he was appointed archdeacon of Canterbury, and displayed considerable talent as a negotiator. That year, Henry II became king, and he accepted the advice of Theobald, archbishop of Canterbury, to appoint Thomas as his chancellor, the first minister of state. Thomas's temperament and interests matched those of Henry, and the two became close friends. They hunted, partied, and even rode into battle together.

right: **Murder of Thomas Becket, 12th-century manuscript**
Becket's murder shocked the Christian world.

Becket's Martyrdom

One of the problems Henry had inherited was an argument with the Pope over the right of the crown to make ecclesiastical appointments. As chancellor, Thomas defended the king's interests. After Archbishop Theobald died in 1161, the king secured the archbishopric of Canterbury for Thomas—an act he soon came to regret. Thomas tried to refuse, but Henry insisted. Their relationship instantly changed: Thomas resigned the chancellorship, gave up hunting and feasting, and adopted an austere way of life. He threw himself wholeheartedly into defending church interests, even when they clashed with those of the king. After a series of confrontations over various issues including "benefit of clergy" (the right of those in holy orders to be tried only in ecclesiastical courts) Henry tried to force Thomas to resign. He refused, and fled the country in 1164.

The argument was continued by correspondence, and Thomas excommunicated two of his disobedient bishops. The pope brokered a reconciliation, but it was superficial. When Thomas returned to England in 1170, there were further clashes, and the king's exasperation was obvious to all, although it is not certain that he actually spoke the words traditionally attributed to him: "Who will rid me of this turbulent priest?" In any event, four of his barons did so, by storming into Canterbury cathedral and hacking Becket to death with their swords.

The assassination outraged Christendom. In 1173 Thomas was canonized, and Henry did public penance by being scourged as he knelt at the saint's tomb. St. Thomas's cult spread rapidly, and his relics were visited by pilgrims from far and wide. Pictures of his martyrdom were painted soon after the event in places as far apart as Iceland, Sicily. and Armenia. More than 700 miracles were reported at his shrine in the ten years that followed his death.

The magnificence of the tomb of St.Thomas the Martyr, archbishop of Canterbury, is that which passes all belief. This, notwithstanding its great size, is entirely covered with plates of pure gold; but the gold is scarcely visible from the variety of precious stones with which it is studded, such as sapphires, diamonds, rubies, balasrubies, and emeralds; and on every side that the eye turns, something more beautiful than the other appears.

A RELATION, OR RATHER A TRUE ACCOUNT, OF THE ISLAND OF ENGLAND,
A VENETIAN DIPLOMAT, C. 1500

The Bonfire of Sanctities

The familiar world of relics, pilgrimages, and *The Golden Legend* was fragmented by the Reformation, in which large parts of Christian Europe rejected the teachings of the Catholic Church and the authority of the Pope. The objection of reformers to many aspects of popular religion, including the cult of saints, sprang from the teaching of Martin Luther (1483–1546) that man is saved by faith alone, not by works.

In the northern European nation states that embraced Protestantism, all veneration of the saints was suppressed, and pilgrimages and processions in their honor were banned. Religious images of any kind were condemned by many Protestant reformers as idolatrous. They were seen as celebrations of man's glory, not God's. In 1522, all the images in the churches of Luther's Wittenberg were destroyed in a riot, and events there were imitated in other German towns. Church statues and stained-glass windows were smashed, wall paintings were covered over in whitewash, and relics were cast onto bonfires, where they were burned alongside liturgical vestments and books. In 1524, the interiors of the two parish churches of the Baltic city of Riga were wrecked. Their altars were destroyed, and their pictures, statues, and relics of the saints heaped up outside the city walls and burned. In 1566, fanatical followers of the reformer John Calvin (1509–64) raged through the whole of the northern Netherlands destroying every religious image they could find.

In England, the Reformation was imposed (and moderated) by the authority of the king through the hierarchy of archbishops and bishops, who had—with the single exception of St. John Fisher (1469–1535)—accepted his claim to be "Supreme Head of the Church of England." His bishop of Salisbury described the cult of relics as an "intolerable superstition and abominable idolatry." In 1538 the bones of St. Thomas Becket at Canterbury cathedral were removed from their reliquary and scattered, and his magnificent shrine broken up and stripped of its ornamentation. It yielded twenty-four cartloads of treasure, all of which was appropriated by King Henry VIII. The same year, the great shrine of Our Lady of Walsingham was destroyed, and its statue taken to London to be publicly burned. Rood screens that separated church sanctuaries from the rest of the building were torn out, and with them, their carved statues of the saints at the foot of the cross, the Virgin Mary, and St. John. In the parish church of Salle, in Norfolk, the reformers who ripped out the rood did so with such angry enthusiasm that their sawmarks are still visible in the stonework.

**Weep, weep O Walsingham,
Whose days are night:
Blessings turned to blasphemies,
Holy deed to spite;
Sin is where Our Lady sate:
Heaven is turned to hell:
Satan sits where Our Lord did sway—
Walsingham, oh, farewell.**

ANONYMOUS, 16TH CENTURY, *LAMENT FOR WALSINGHAM*,

Today's Pilgrims

The Reformation did not reach every part of Christendom, and pilgrims continued to make their way to the shrines of the Catholic world. They still do: today, the most popular destinations include places where apparitions of the Blessed Virgin Mary have taken place. Over the years, numerous such appearances have been reported, but the church regards only a few of them as genuine.

One of those recognized by the church is the Mexican shrine of Guadalupe, where in 1531 the Virgin appeared to an Indian convert called Juan Diego. The story says that she told him to take some roses to the bishop: he gathered them in his cloak. When he opened it, a picture of the Virgin had been miraculously imprinted on it. The image is now displayed in the basilica. St. Juan Diego was canonized in 2002 by Pope John Paul II, who made three visits to Guadalupe. The shrine receives ten million pilgrims every year.

The world's second most visited Catholic shrine is the tomb of the stigmatic Padre Pio (1887–1968) at San Giovanni Rotondo in the south of Italy. About seven million pilgrims arrive annually. Five million a year visit Lourdes in the French Pyrenees, where the Virgin appeared in 1858 to 14-year-old St. Bernadette Soubirous (1844–79). Many of them are sick or dying, and numerous miraculous cures have been recorded.

previous page: **Pilgrims to the Shrine of Our Lady of Walsingham, Norfolk, England, 1930's**
The pilgrimage to the shrine that Henry VIII destroyed was revived in 1897.
left: **Statue of Our Lady of Guadalupe, Zihuatanejo, Mexico**
Our Lady of Guadalupe is the patron saint of Mexico.

LES HAUTES-PYRÉNÉES

The Shrine at Fatima

Five million pilgrims arrive annually at the Portuguese shrine of Fatima, where in 1917 the Virgin Mary appeared to ten-year-old Lucia dos Santos and her two cousins, nine-year-old Francisco Marto and his sister, Jacinta, aged seven. The Virgin entrusted the children with three "secrets." The first two were later interpreted as predictions of the sufferings caused by atheistic communism and the Second World War; the last was interpreted as describing an assassination attempt upon the Pope. John Paul II was shot in St. Peter's Square 13 May 1981, the anniversary of the first of the Fatima apparitions. After his recovery, he placed one of the bullets that had been fired at him in the crown of the statue at Fatima. Francisco and Jacinta died in 1919 and 1920, and were beatified in the year 2000. Lucia died in 2005.

I love Our Lord so much! At times, I seem to have a fire in my heart, but it does not burn me.

BLESSED JACINTA MARTO

previous page: **Postcard of the grotto of Massabielle, Lourdes, early 20th century, French**
The crutches are left by people healed at the shrine.
right: **Postcard of the visionary children of Fatima, c. 1917, Portuguese**
From left to right are Jacinta, Francisco, and Lucia.

JACINTA   FRANCISCO   LUCIA

The Shrine at Knock

One-and-a-half million pilgrims a year travel to the Irish shrine of Knock, where in 1879, 15 people aged from five to seventy-five saw figures of the Virgin Mary, St. Joseph, St. John the Apostle, and a lamb on a plain altar appear over the gable of the village chapel. And a million visit the miraculous icon of the Virgin of Czestochowa in the Jasna Góra monastery in Poland. Tradition describes it as the work of St. Luke, though modern scholarship doubts this. If St. Luke did paint an icon of the Virgin, this could perhaps be a copy of it—in any event, it is an image of inspirational pathos and beauty. Most contemporary pilgrims use modern methods of travel, but a number still walk the 175 miles (280 km.) from Warsaw to Jasna Góra.

The other medieval pilgrimage that many make on foot is to the apostle's tomb at Santiago de Compostela. Some make the journey exactly as people would have done in the Middle Ages—by starting their walk at their own front doors. The Archbishop of Santiago awards a certificate to all those who can prove they have completed at least the last 60 miles (100 km) of the journey on foot, or 120 miles (200 km) by bicycle. Most pilgrims do very much more than that. Not all today's pilgrims are motivated by instincts of traditional religion. More claim to make the journey for "spiritual" than for religious reasons, and some simply regard it as an inexpensive walking or cycling holiday. Nearly all, though, report that they find the journey uplifting.

Give me my scallop-shell of quiet,
My staff of faith to walk upon,
My scrip of joy, immortal diet,
My bottle of salvation,
My gown of glory, hope's true gage,
And thus I'll take my pilgrimage.

SIR WALTER RALEIGH, *THE PASSIONATE MAN'S PILGRIMAGE*

When you look in you would say it is the
abode of saints, so brilliantly does it shine
on all sides with gems, gold and silver ...
Our Lady stands in the dark at the right side
of the altar ... a little image, remarkable
neither for its size, material or workmanship.

ERASMUS DESCRIBES THE SHRINE OF OUR LADY OF WALSINGHAM, 1513

[King Henry II] set out with a sad heart to
the tomb of St. Thomas at Canterbury ...
he walked barefoot and clad in a woollen
smock all the way to the martyr's tomb.
There he lay and of his free will was
whipped by all the bishops and abbots
there present and each individual monk of
the church of Canterbury.

GERVASE OF CANTERBURY, GESTA REGUM (c.1210)

To the tomb of blessed James the sick come and are healed, the blind are given light, the crippled raised up, the demon-possessed are set free, the sorrowful are consoled, and, what is best of all, the prayers of the faithful are heard: therefore, foreign folk from every part of the world, hasten in great numbers, bearing gifts of praise to the Lord, Alleluia.

CODEX CALIXTINUS, 12TH CENTURY

Through the night of doubt and sorrow
Onward goes the pilgrim band,
Singing songs of expectation,
Marching to the Promised Land.

SABINE BARING-GOULD

Then fancies flee away!
I'll fear not what men say,
I'll labor night and day
To be a pilgrim.

JOHN BUNYAN

chapter 6
Holiness and Orders

Monastic Rules

The majority of the saints in the calendar are members of religious orders or secular clergy, whose lives were consecrated to the service of God. The first religious order was the group of communities living under the direction of St. Pachomius (292–346). The guidelines that he drew up for his monasteries influenced the monastic rules drawn up by St. Basil the Great (c. 330–79), which is still followed by Greek Orthodox monks and nuns today. Basil, bishop of Caesarea, gave his inheritance to the poor and distributed welfare to the hungry. He founded a new town—Basiliad—with a hospital as well as a church and was an accomplished preacher and champion of orthodoxy.

The bread you store up belongs to the hungry; the cloak that lies in your chest belongs to the naked; the gold that you have hidden in the ground belongs to the poor.

ST. BASIL THE GREAT

previous page: **Painting by Walter Tyndale in Horatio F. Brown's *Dalmatia*, 1925, English**
One monk reads while another draws water from the well in the cloisters of the monastery of San Francesco at Ragusa (now Dubrovnik) Croatia.
next page: **St. Benedict Presents the Rule of the New Order, 1390-1427, Italian**
St. Benedict's rules have become the leading guide to monastic life.

The Order of St. Benedict

The monastic regimes of both Basil and Pachomius were inspirations for the rule drawn up by St. Benedict of Nursia (c. 480–550). Benedict began his religious life as a hermit at Subiaco, near Tivoli in Italy. When others gathered around him, he organized them into groups and appointed an abbot for each. He then took a group of monks with him to Monte Cassino, near Naples, where he founded a monastery that has survived to this day, though it had to be rebuilt after its destruction during the Second World War.

Benedict's rule is moderate and humane, and provides for an orderly life of prayer and spiritual reading balanced by physical work. The celebrated French preacher Bishop Bossuet (1627–1704) called it "an epitome of Christianity, a learned and mysterious abridgement of all the doctrines of the Gospel, all the institutions of the Fathers, and all the counsels of perfection."

Let the oratory be what it is called, and let nothing else be done or stored there. When the Work of God is finished, let all go out with the deepest silence, and let reverence be shown to God.

FROM *THE RULE OF ST. BENEDICT*

The Cistercians

The Rule of St. Benedict was adopted across western Europe, and monasteries flourished. In 1098, St. Robert of Molesme (1027–1110) founded the monastery of Citeaux, near Dijon. Citeaux gave its name to the Cistercians, a reformed order of monks (and, later, nuns.) The Cistercians flourished under the leadership of St. Bernard (c. 1090–1153), abbot of Clairvaux (near Dijon), who established daughter houses all over the continent. By the end of the thirteenth century, 680 Cistercian abbeys had been founded.

Bernard's influence extended far beyond the monastic world. He drew up the rules for the newly formed Order of Knights Templar in 1128. He campaigned to have Innocent II recognized as pope after the disputed election of 1130, and was invited by Pope Eugenius III to call Christian Europe to arms for the Second Crusade (1147–9), though the campaign itself was a complete failure. He was a fierce opponent of the independent-minded scholar Peter Abelard (1079–1142), but he was also the gentle author of the mystical classic *The Love of God*. His appreciation of the physical reality of the incarnate God and his mother contributed significantly to the development of medieval spirituality.

right: **St. Bernard of Clairvaux, 19th-century engraving, Pilgeram and Lefèvre after Turpin de Crisse, French**
By the time St. Bernard died, there were nearly 400 Cistercian houses in Europe.

The Carthusians

St. Bruno (c. 1032–1101) introduced a more radical form of monasticism when he founded the Carthusians in 1084. The order takes its name from La Grande Chartreuse in the French Alps, where he built a chapel surrounded by individual cells in an arrangement that imitates the clusters of desert hermits in third- and fourth-century Egypt and Palestine. Carthusians live in solitude, meeting only for prayer, and sharing meals only on feast days. English Carthusian monasteries are called "Charterhouses," an Anglicization of *Chartreuse*.

King Henry II invited St. Hugh of Lincoln (c. 1140–1200) to leave the Grande Chartreuse for England, to become prior of the Charterhouse that he had founded in reparation for the murder of St. Thomas of Canterbury. After Hugh had revived its fortunes, he was invited to become bishop of Lincoln, a post he accepted only under obedience. Despite his reluctance, he was a model bishop. He fostered learning, rebuilt his cathedral, looked after lepers, and defended the rights of the church against the political interests of three kings.

The silent courts, where night and day
Into their stone-carved basins cold
The splashing icy fountains play—
The humid corridors behold!
Where, ghostlike in the deepening night,
Cowl'd forms rush by in gleaming white.

MATTHEW ARNOLD, *THE GRANDE CHARTREUSE*

above: **St. Hugo in the Refectory of the Carthusians,
Francisco de Zurbaran, 1633, Spanish**

St. Hugo gave St. Bruno the land for his monastery.

The Mendicant Orders

Two saints of the thirteenth century created a new kind of religious order. The followers of the Italian St. Francis of Assisi (1181–1226) and the Spaniard St. Dominic Guzmán (c. 1170–1221) were called mendicants, because they supported themselves by begging for alms. They owned no property, either individually or in common. They were not monks, but friars; they did not live in monasteries, but in the world. The two orders reflect the very different personalities of their founders. Dominic was an ecclesiastical statesman, who was at home in the corridors of power; Francis was not at home in this world at all. Dominic was an intellectual defender of orthodoxy; Francis had little regard for book learning, and thought with his heart.

A man who governs his passions is master of his world. We must either command them or be enslaved by them.

ST. DOMINIC

left: **St. Dominic, Sandro Botticelli, 1444–1510, Italian**
The order founded by St. Dominic in 1215 is formally known as the "Order of Preachers," and Dominic had been a formidable preacher himself. He spent 10 years attempting to convert the Cathars, the heretical sect that was later put down so mercilessly by the Albigensian crusade. One of the emblems that identifies him in art is a dog—a pun on the Latin words *Domini canes*, "dogs of the Lord."

The Franciscans

Francis (1181–1226) was the son of a wealthy merchant. As a young man, he enjoyed the pleasures that wealth brings, but in his early twenties he experienced a conversion that led him to embrace absolute poverty. Praying in the half-derelict church of San Damiano, he heard the voice of Christ speaking to him from the crucifix: "Francis, go and repair my house, for it is falling into ruin." Understanding the words to refer to the building, Francis set about restoring it. Shortly afterward, he renounced all his worldly possessions in a dramatic public gesture, throwing his money and clothes to the ground in front of the bishop. He then spent two years wandering the countryside, praying, preaching, and tending to lepers.

Gradually, an informal brotherhood gathered about him. Stories about his exploits abounded, and many of them are well known even today. He preached to the birds at Bevagna; he tamed the wolf that terrorized the townsfolk of Gubbio; in Greccio, he set up the first Christmas crib, with a live ox and ass. But there was a tough side to Francis, too. In 1219, he traveled to Syria, walked through the Saracen lines, and demanded to be taken to the Sultan so that he could appeal to him directly to accept the truths of Christianity. The Sultan was impressed, but unconvinced. Francis was so determined that neither he nor his followers should own any property that when someone referred to a rough shelter of sticks as "his," he refused to use it any longer.

right: **St. Francis, Francesco Francia (Francesco Raibolini), 1450–1517, Italian**
The unworldly St. Francis is widely admired by non-Christians.

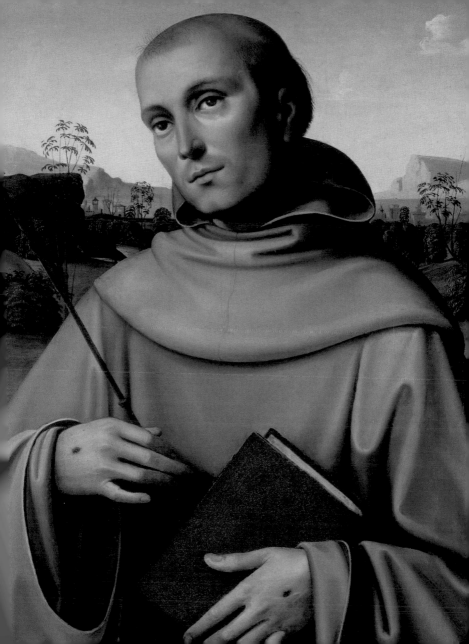

When Francis found that the citizens of Assisi had given a house to his friars, he climbed onto the roof and tore off the tiles with his own hands. This absolute refusal to own any temporal possessions might easily have led Francis and his companions to be condemned as heretics, like the Waldensians and the Cathars, who rejected the authority of the church as vehemently as they rejected personal property; but Pope Innocent III recognized that Francis was different. He did not challenge the doctrines of the church but wanted the church's approval to teach those doctrines by example. The pope gave it.

Touched by his example, St Clare (1194–1253), another wealthy inhabitant of Assisi, became a nun and founded a contemplative order that embraced the Franciscan spirit, the Poor Clares. Francis' band of followers was expanding, but he was reluctant to establish a detailed rule for them; he wanted them to be governed not by regulations, but by the love of God. But if his movement was to outlive him, it would need a formal constitution. In 1220, Francis resigned as Minister General, and—under obedience—he moderated their rule.

After his death, it was to be moderated further. In 1245, Pope Innocent IV declared that the followers of the man who had wanted them to own nothing might enjoy the use of anything, provided that its legal ownership was vested in the papacy. Francis did not want his spiritual family (called *minores*) to accept ecclesiastical preferment. He himself was not even a priest, but soon there were Franciscan bishops, cardinals and even popes.

left: **St. Bernardino and St. Catherine of Siena, Carlo Crivelli (Donatino Creti), c. 1470–1495, Italian**
St. Bernardino was a Franciscan friar; St. Catherine, a Dominican tertiary.

Carmelites and Ursulines

An Englishman, St. Simon Stock (d. 1265) effectively established a third order of mendicant friars by reorganizing the Carmelites. The order had originated in a community of desert hermits gathered on Mount Carmel in Palestine. Under St. Simon's direction, Carmelite spirituality was disseminated through the universities: he founded houses at Oxford, Cambridge, Paris, and Bologna. After a period of decline in the fifteenth century, the Carmelites were revived, in Spain, by St. Theresa of Ávila (1515–82) and St. John of the Cross (1542–91). Together, they established a reformed branch of the order called Discalced ("barefoot") Carmelites that restored the tradition of contemplative prayer. One of its best-known members was St. Theresa of Lisieux (1873–97) whose life of simple piety is known to the world through her spiritual autobiography, *The Story of a Soul*.

The decline of the religious orders into comfort and corruption was one of the causes of the Reformation. The Counter Reformation was unable to repair this breach in western Christianity, but it did produce a number of new religious orders. St. Angela Merici (1474–1540) founded the Ursulines to provide education for poor girls. St. Cajetan (1480–1547) established the Theatines to counteract the clerical laxity of the time. These orders were a living refutation of Luther's doctrine that salvation was by faith alone: they were active, rather than contemplative; the fruits of their faith were good works.

right: **Carmelite nuns by unnamed artist in Rev. Charles Warren Currier's *History of Religious Orders*, 1896, American**
The first Carmelites were pilgrims who became desert hermits.

The Abbot should employ the utmost solicitude, and take care with all prudence and diligence, lest he lose any of the sheep entrusted to him. For he should know that he has undertaken the care of weak souls, not the tyranny over the strong.

RULE OF ST. BENEDICT

This is the rule and way of life of the friars minor: to observe the holy gospel of our Lord Jesus Christ, living in obedience, without personal possessions, and in chastity.

THE RULE OF ST. FRANCIS, 1223

The best preparation for prayer is to read the lives of the saints...

ST. PHILIP NERI

Living in a community is like life in the arena: you are continuously stretched to perform better.

ST. JOHN OF THE CROSS

Be gentle to all and stern with yourself.

ST. TERESA OF AVILA

Jesuits and Oratorians

The greatest of the Counter-Reformation religious orders was the Society of Jesus, which was founded in 1534 by the Spanish nobleman St. Ignatius of Loyola (1491–1556). Ignatius had been a soldier who took a vow to "serve only God and the Roman pontiff, His vicar on earth" while recovering from a traumatic injury sustained in the field of battle. He organized his spiritual troops with military precision. Rigorously disciplined in spirituality and obedience, they became influential scientists, theologians, poets, philosophers, pastors, preachers, and educators. They also gave tremendous impetus to the missions in the Americas and the Far East. From a base established in Goa, St. Francis Xavier (1506–52) traveled tirelessly through Asia with the vigor of a second St. Paul, establishing Christian communities from southern India to Japan. Canonized by Gregory XV in 1622, he was declared patron saint of foreign missions by Pius XI in 1927.

One of St. Francis Xavier's admirers was the Florentine St. Philip Neri (1515–95), who originally wanted to follow his example and work overseas, but who was persuaded to conduct his religious work in Rome, where he founded the Congregation of the Oratory.

The Oratorians are not, strictly speaking, a religious order, but an association of priests sharing a common life. They do not take a vow of poverty. Philip was a popular figure, whose sense of humor and sympathetic personality won him many friends and admirers. He was also a gifted confessor, who led an intense interior life. He would frequently experience ecstasies while saying mass; they would sometimes last for hours. St. Philip cultivated the beauty of holiness, and the services celebrated in his oratories have always been characterized by dignity and musical excellence.

Dearest Jesus, teach us to
    be generous;
To serve Thee as Thou deservest;
To give, and not to count the cost;
To fight, and not to heed the wounds;
To toil, and not to seek for rest;
To labor, and to seek for no reward,
Save that of knowing that we do
    Thy holy will.

PRAYER OF ST. IGNATIUS LOYOLA

St. Vincent de Paul

St. Vincent de Paul (1581–1660) founded the Congregation of Priests of the Mission, known as the Lazarists (after the Parisian church of Saint-Lazare) or the Vincentians (after his own name). He also established the Sisters of Charity. Their purpose was to minister to the poor. He was tireless in their service, and used his charm and influence with the aristocracy to persuade them to help him in his efforts. He raised funds for war victims, ransomed galley slaves, and founded hospitals. He was canonized by Clement XII in 1737, and named by Leo XIII as patron saint of charitable societies.

It is our duty to prefer the service of the poor to everything else, and to offer such service as quickly as possible. If a needy person requires medicine or other help during prayer time, do whatever has to be done with peace of mind. Offer the deed to God as your prayer.

ST. VINCENT DE PAUL

previous page: **Death of St. Francis Xavier, 18th-century carving, artist unknown**
St. Francis Xavier died exhausted by his missionary work.
right: **St. Vincent de Paul, Claudius Jacquand, 1805–78, French**
The saint invites offerings for the poor.

Saintly Prelates

Many saints have been secular or diocesan priests, that is, priests who are not members of religious orders, but who work under the direction of a bishop; numerous bishops have been saints, too—though many more have not. St. Athanasius (c. 296–373) was patriarch of Alexandria at a time when Christianity was threatened by the spread of the Arian heresy, whose adherents included many of the bishops of the day. Arianism denied the full divinity of Christ; if it had triumphed, as it seemed likely to, Christianity would have been rendered pointless and the church would inevitably have collapsed. That neither of these things happened is largely due to the efforts of Athanasius. Arianism was condemned at the Council of Nicaea in 325, but it continued to be taught by many bishops. Athanasius argued fearlessly against them, and was deposed and exiled five times as a result.

St. John Chrysostom (347–407) was appointed archbishop of Constantinople at the behest of Emperor Arcadius (377–408), but he immediately made himself unpopular with the establishment by giving to the poor the funds that had previously been spent on entertainment, and by preaching against the immorality of the age. In doing so he made an enemy of the high-living wife of the emperor, and she and other disaffected bishops conspired to have him deposed.

St. Augustine (354–430) was bishop of Hippo (in what is now Tunisia). He was a gifted preacher and a brilliant theologian, whose writings include his own spiritual autobiography, *The Confessions.* In his youth he was given to the pleasures of this world, and fathered a son; his much-quoted prayer of the time was "Lord, make me chaste—but not yet." He and his son Adeodatus were baptized by St. Ambrose (339–97), bishop of Milan.

Ambrose's rise to authority in the church was extraordinary. He was a lawyer; during a public meeting to elect a successor to the bishop that had just died, he spoke up to appeal for calm. A voice from the crowd called, "Ambrose for bishop!" and the cry was taken up. He was not a priest; he was not even baptized—but he was persuaded to accept the appointment, and he was christened, ordained and consecrated bishop within days.

Twelve hundred years later, another saintly prelate presided in Milan. The nephew of Pope Pius IV, St. Charles Borromeo (1538–84) was only twenty-six years old when he was appointed archbishop of what had become a diocese of a thousand parishes. He was a model reformer in the spirit of the Council of Trent (1545–63), to which he was a major contributor. He introduced Sunday schools for the laity, and seminaries to improve the education of priests.

He restored dignity to public worship and distributed his personal fortune to the poor. He acted with great personal courage during an outbreak of the plague, organizing and participating in the care of the sick. His reforms of the clergy made him unpopular with some religious orders; one disgruntled member of the Humiliati (an order suppressed in 1571) attempted to assassinate him in his own chapel.

St. Augustine's Holy Canons

Like many early bishops, St. Augustine had established a community of secular priests that lived under his authority at his cathedral. They were known as "canons." They lived and prayed together, and led an active pastoral life in the wider community. The principles on which he organized them became known as the Rule of St. Augustine, and papal reforms of the clergy during the eleventh and twelfth centuries led to that rule being widely adopted. Soon, there were hundreds of houses of "regular" (i.e., rule-following) canons across Europe. Saints who have been canons of St. Augustine, include St. Lawrence O'Toole (1128–80), archbishop of Dublin; St. Gilbert of Sempringham (1083–1189), English founder of the Gilbertine order of priests, lay brothers, and nuns; and St. Thorlak (1133–93), bishop of Skalholt, Iceland.

Perhaps the best-known Augustinian house today is the monastery in the Great St. Bernard Pass between France and Italy. The place (and its mountain rescue dogs) are named after its founder, St Bernard of Aosta (d. 1081), who established hospices to care for pilgrims crossing the Alps. Bernard was not an Augustinian canon himself, but a secular priest who was a tireless vicar general of his diocese. He was named patron saint of mountaineers by Pope Pius XI in 1923.

left: **Illustration by unnamed artist from the magazine *Le Petit Journal*, October 19th 1913, French**
Monks in St Bernard's monastery have a long tradition of looking after exhausted migrating swallows, which they shelter until fit enough to travel.
next page: **Vision of St. Augustine, Vittore Carpaccio, c. 1455–1526, Italian**
St Augustine has a vision in which St. Jerome warns him of his imminent death.

Canonized Popes

Of the 264 popes before Benedict XVI, seventy-three have been saints. Popes who have been canonized include Gregory the Great (c. 540–604), the Apostle of the English, who called himself "the servant of the servants of God," a title that popes have used ever since. St. Pius V (1504–72) put into effect the decrees of the Council of Trent, restored liturgical rites, published a catechism that was widely translated, and put an end to absentee bishops. His reign saw the victory of the Battle of Lepanto (1571), which saved Christendom from Ottoman domination, but his intervention in English politics was less successful.

Excommunicating Queen Elizabeth I and absolving her Catholic subjects from allegiance to her made their situation worse, allowing them to be demonized as traitors. The reforms of St. Pius X (1835–1914) included the encouragement of frequent communion and the restoration of the church's traditional musical heritage, Gregorian chant.

The Pope was in his chapel before day or battle broke,
(Don John of Austria is hidden in the smoke.)
The hidden room in man's house where God sits all the year,
The secret window whence the world looks small and
> **very dear.**

GK CHESTERTON, *LEPANTO*

right: **Pope Gregory and the Angles, Kronheim print in *Pictures of English History from the Earliest Times*, c. 1892, English**
St. Gregory, seeing English slave children in Rome, says, "*Non Angli, sed angeli!*" —"They are not Angles, but angels!"

Holy Priests

The patron saint of parish priests is St. Jean-Baptiste Vianney (1786–1859), who is better known as the Curé d'Ars. His saintliness was widely recognized in his own lifetime: 20,000 people a year came to his simple country church near Lyons to hear him preach and to go to him for confession. It was a remarkable achievement for someone who had been known as the least academically gifted student at his seminary. He frequently spent all day in the confessional, where he earned a reputation for being able to read hearts and discern unconfessed sins. He was associated with numerous miracles, ranging from healing the sick to obtaining money for his charitable works. He was canonized by Pius XI in 1925.

The Greek saints Cyril and Methodius (c. 815–85) share the same feast day because they were brothers, who worked together as missionary priests. Their joint efforts in Moravia did much to evangelize the Slavs, for whom they translated the Scriptures and liturgy into Slavonic. Cyril invented an alphabet in which to write them; its later form became known as "Cyrillic." The use of the vernacular language in the liturgy was then controversial, and involved them in political as well as doctrinal difficulties. It was seen as encouraging nationalism, and challenging the unifying influence of the Holy Roman Empire.

Other missionaries from Germany had been much less successful in Moravia, and the German hierarchy obstructed Cyril's and Methodius's efforts. The brothers were summoned to Rome to account for themselves, but they were well received, and the pope made them both bishops. After Cyril died in 869, the pope sent Methodius back to Moravia, and created for him an archdiocese independent of German influence. The German hierarchy deposed and imprisoned him; the pope only got him released two years later. Once again, he was denounced, and summoned to Rome to answer his accusers; once again, he was cleared of charges of heresy and disobedience.

Today Cyril and Methodius are seen as symbols of unity rather than division; they are honored by Eastern and Western Christians equally, and were nominated patrons of Europe (jointly with St. Benedict) by Pope John Paul II.

... We pray Thee, Lord, give to us, Thy servants, in all time of our life on earth, a mind forgetful of past ill-will, a pure conscience and sincere thoughts, and a heart to love our brethren; for the sake of Jesus Christ, Thy Son, our Lord and only Saviour.

FROM THE COPTIC LITURGY OF SAINT CYRIL

St. Thomas Aquinas

St. Thomas Aquinas (c. 1225–74) was a Dominican friar, though his aristocratic parents were unhappy with his decision to become a mendicant. They tried everything they could think of to dissuade him, including kidnapping him, imprisoning him, and sending a prostitute to tempt him from his priestly vocation. Their efforts failed, though, and he went on to become the order's greatest saint after its founder, and the greatest theologian in the history of the Catholic church.

His mind dominated medieval scholasticism. His intellectual abilities were astonishing; it was said that he could dictate to four secretaries at once. He studied and taught at universities in Italy and France, where he was befriended by the king, St. Louis IX. He wrote his vast *Summa Theologica* "to convey the content of the Christian religion in a way fit for the training of beginners"; it quickly became a standard textbook in the universities of Christendom. The *Summa* is a comprehensive exposition of Christian theology, in which the teachings of the church are presented, and objections to them noted and refuted. In 1272 Aquinas experienced a mystical vision; he said that his writings were "as straw" compared to what he had seen in it, and he wrote no more. He was canonized by Pope John XXII in 1323 and proclaimed a Doctor of the Church by Pope Pius V in 1567.

right: Reproduction of painting by Jean Fouquet, in Léon Curmer, ***Oeuvre de Jehan Foucquet*, 1865, French**
St. Thomas Aquinas is often referred to as "the Angelic Doctor." A contemporary described him as "tall, upright, large and well-built, with a complexion like ripe wheat, and whose head had grown bald early."

St. Katharine Drexel

The story of St. Katharine Drexel (1858–1955) shows that, even if it is easier for a camel to go through the eye of a needle than for a rich man to enter the kingdom of God, it is not impossible to get to Heaven if you are a wealthy nun. Daughter of a Philadelphia banker and philanthropist, Katharine Drexel inherited a fortune on his death when she was twenty-seven, and spent it—and the rest of her life—in the service of the poorest and most disadvantaged people in the United States.

In 1887, she founded the St. Catherine Indian School in Santa Fe, New Mexico. Shortly afterward, on a visit to Pope Leo XIII in Rome, she asked him to send missionaries to work in some of the Native American missions that she supported. The pope suggested that she become a missionary herself. She was surprised, but accepted the advice, recognizing that he had identified her calling. In 1889 she began her training in religious life with the Sisters of Mercy at Pittsburgh, nursing the sick in their hospital. In 1891 she professed her first vows as a religious, and founded the Sisters of the Blessed Sacrament for Indians and Colored People, an order dedicated to sharing with them the gifts of the Gospel and the Eucharist. It is now known as the Sisters of the Blessed Sacrament.

Katharine Drexel was a fierce critic of social and racial injustice long before such issues were widely acknowledged, and was particularly moved by the material and educational poverty of minorities. She founded nearly sixty schools and missions, mostly in the west and southwest United States, where her sisters engaged in social work, hospital visiting and teaching. In 1925, she founded Xavier University of Louisiana, the only predominantly Afro-American

Catholic institution of higher learning in the United States. Katharine was admired for her personal holiness as well as for her boundless energy. Incapacitated by illness for the last eighteen years of her life, and having spent all her inherited wealth on others, she used the time that remained to her in adoration, contemplation, and prayer. The heiress who had spent nothing on herself was beatified by Pope John Paul II on November 20th 1980, and canonized by him in a ceremony in St. Peter's Square, Rome on October 1st 2000.

If we wish to serve God and love our neighbor well, we must manifest our joy in the service that we render to Him and to them. Let us open wide our hearts. It is Joy which invites us. Press forward and fear nothing.

ST. KATHARINE DREXEL

It is better to illuminate than merely to shine, to deliver to others contemplated truths than merely to contemplate.

ST. THOMAS AQUINAS

My congregation is my family; its members are my parents, my brothers and sisters, and my children. They are dearer to me than light; the rays of the sun are dark compared with the rays of their love. Indeed, their love is weaving for me a crown that I shall wear for all eternity.

ST. JOHN CHRYSOSTOM

Jesus whom I know as my Redeemer cannot be less than God.

ST. ATHANASIUS

It is a greater thing to resist the enemy inside you than the one far off.

ST. AMBROSE OF MILAN

You know well enough that Our Lord does not look so much at the greatness of our actions, nor even at their difficulty, but at the love with which we do them.

ST. THÉRÈSE OF LISIEUX

REX BI H

chapter 7

Royalty and Commoners

Lay Saints

Many people find it difficult to believe that laymen and laywomen can become saints. The Second Vatican Council (1963–5) reaffirmed that Christians "of whatever rank or status" are called to holiness, and Pope John Paul II, in his Apostolic Letter *Novo Millennio Ineunte* of 2001, thanked God for enabling him to beatify and canonize "many lay people who attained holiness in the most ordinary circumstances of life." But that very year, the Secretary of the Congregation for the Causes of Saints felt it necessary to refute what he described as a "popular belief": that "only priests and sisters could become saints."

One reason for this belief is that lay saints are outnumbered by sainted priests, monks, and nuns. This is partly explained by the fact that religious orders have the time and energy to push for their saintly members to be recognized. Another reason is a tendency to think that only people who lead a formally ordained or consecrated life can be expected to achieve absolute holiness. The error of that assumption is demonstrated by the existence of countless lay saints.

There were laymen and laywomen among the very first saints. The married couple SS. Priscilla and Aquila, Jewish tentmakers converted to Christianity who became co-workers of St. Paul, are mentioned several times in the New Testament.

previous page: **Detail from the Bayeux Tapestry, 11th century, Norman**
Edward the Confessor is always shown tall, thin and bearded.
right: **St. Prisca, whose legend merges with St. Priscilla, engraving, undated, unnamed artist**
In Prisca's legendary martyrdom, the lions refused to harm her.

St. Paul (in Romans 16) says that SS. Priscilla and Aquila risked their lives to save him. SS. Felicity and Perpetua (both martyred in 203) were also married. Perpetua already had a child; Felicity's was born during her imprisonment.

Many other ancient martyrs were layfolk. According to the *Ecclesiastical History of the English People* of St. Bede (673–735), the third-century martyr St. Alban, who gave his name to the English town where his relics were buried, was a Roman citizen. He was a pagan who sheltered a hunted Christian priest during a period of persecution. The priest converted him, and both were caught and killed.

Bede does not record Alban's profession, but we do know that numbers of the early martyrs were soldiers. St. Marinus (d. c. 260) had enjoyed a successful career in the army before he was denounced as a Christian by a jealous colleague. He was given three hours to decide whether to sacrifice to the gods or be executed. He chose death. St. Marcellus, who died in about 298, was a centurion. During a public festival in honor of the emperors Diocletian and Maximian, he threw down his badges of allegiance, and made a dramatic proclamation of his faith: "I am a soldier of Jesus Christ, the eternal king, and from now on I cease to serve your emperors and I despise the worship of your gods of wood and stone." St. Maximilian (d. 295) was the son of a soldier, but when he was called up he refused to serve. His *Acts* record the interview in which he says, "I will not be a soldier of this world, because I am a soldier of God." St. Julius (d. 304) was a distinguished veteran whom the prefect Maximus was clearly reluctant to execute. He offered him extra pay if he would only sacrifice to the gods, but Julius replied "I have chosen death that I might live with the saints for ever."

Though the majority of lay saints have been martyrs, there have been numerous lay confessors, too. The Spaniards SS. Isidore the Farmer (c. 1080–1130) and María de la Cabeza (d. c. 1175) were married to each other, and had a son. Isidore was a farmworker, who dedicated his whole life to prayer, including the time he spent working in the field. The English St. Walstan (who is believed to have died in the early eleventh century) was also a farmworker who achieved holiness in a humble lay state. His shrine in the Norfolk village of Bawburgh was a center of local pilgrimage in the Middle Ages. St. Walstan had a reputation for providing miraculous cures, including—remarkably—restoring the severed genitals of men and beasts. It was one of the more eccentric aspects of the folklore of fertility that grew up around this saint of the fields, whose real history is buried beneath colorful legends.

**You knight of Christ, Walstan holy,
Our cry to thee meekly we pray.
Shield us from mischief, sorrow and folly,
Engendring and renewing from day to day**

FROM *LIVES OF ST. WALSTAN*

next page: **The Last Chapter, James Doyle Penrose, 1832–1900, Irish**
The Venerable Bede's *Ecclesiastical History of the English People* contains the dramatic story of St. Alban's martyrdom.

75

A Living Tradition

There are many examples of modern lay saints. Blessed Frederick Ozanam (1813–53) had a successful secular career as an academic, was happily married, and had a daughter. When a student at the Sorbonne, he took part in public debates in which he and others argued against agnostic and atheistic speakers. It was not for this that he was beatified in 1997, but for his extraordinary works of charity. He was moved to them by a question put to him by one of his debating opponents, who asked him what he actually *did* to demonstrate the faith that he so freely talked about. The barb struck home, and Ozanam began to visit and help the poor, giving them food, clothing, and firewood that he paid for from his own pocket. He later recruited others to form what was to become the international charitable organisation, the Society of St. Vincent de Paul. One of his friends told Pope Pius IX that he felt that Ozanam was so gifted and good that he should have become a priest, and that it was a pity that he had "fallen into the trap" of marriage. "What?" the pope replied. "I thought that Our Lord established seven sacraments, not six sacraments and a trap!"

The Italian doctor St. Joseph Moscati (1880–1927) was a practical as well as a spiritual hero: he rescued many patients from a hospital destroyed by the eruption of Mount Vesuvius in 1906, and saved many more lives during the cholera epidemic of 1911. That same year, he became a professor of chemical physiology at the University of Naples. Shortly afterward, he made a private vow of chastity. He wanted to become a Jesuit priest, but was persuaded that his true vocation was in medicine. He worked tirelessly for the poor, from whom he took no payment for his services, and to whom he gave spiritual as well as medical help. He was canonized in 1987.

St. Maria Goretti (1890–1902) was only a child when she was mortally stabbed by a neighbor, Alessandro Serenelli, as she resisted his attempts to rape her. She forgave Serenelli on her deathbed; he was sentenced to life imprisonment but released after twenty-seven years, a reformed man. He attributed his repentance to Maria's intercession. She was canonized by Pius XII in 1950. Her mother was present at the ceremony. In the year of his own death Serenelli said, "I killed a saint, and now after sixty-nine years of penance and prayer, by God's mercy I am going to join her in Heaven."

Man is not merely a combination of appetites, instincts, passions and curiosity. Something more is needed to explain great human deeds, virtues, sacrifices, martyrdom. There is an element in the great mystics, the saints, the prophets, whose influence has been felt for centuries, which escapes mere intelligence.

LECOMTE DU NOUY, *HUMAN DESTINY*

The churches of Asia salute you. Aquila and Priscilla salute you much in the Lord, with the church that is in their house.

1 CORINTHIANS 16:19

Lord Jesus Christ, I suffer this for your name. I beg you to receive my spirit together with your holy martyrs.

ST. JULIUS

Charity must never look to the past, but always to the future, because the number of its past works is still very small and the present and future miseries that it must alleviate are infinite.

BLESSED FREDERIC OZANAM

The blessed Alban suffered death on the twenty-second day of June, near the city of Verulam ... where afterwards, when peaceable Christian times were restored, a church of wonderful workmanship, and altogether worthy to commemorate his martyrdom, was erected. In which place the cure of sick persons and the frequent working of wonders cease not to this day.

BEDE, ECCLESIASTICAL HISTORY

If beast also in sickness should fall
That man's labor better should be
In Walstan's name, man, to God do call:
A ready remedy thou shalt soon see.

LIVES OF ST WALSTAN

Sanctity and Monarchy

Numerous kings and queens have been saints. St. Ethelbert of Kent (560–616) welcomed St. Augustine of Canterbury (d. c. 604) and his companions sent by Pope St. Gregory the Great (c. 540–604) in 597, and became a Christian himself four years later, supporting Augustine in his work, and building a monastery near Canterbury. St. Oswald (c. 605–42) was king of Northumbria. He was killed in battle by the pagan king Penda of Mercia, who butchered his body and hung his head and limbs up on poles in honor of the Norse god, Woden. The large number of relics that resulted contributed significantly to the spread of his cult.

A second St. Ethelbert (779–94) was king of the East Angles. It seems that the motives behind his assassination were political, but he was nevertheless widely venerated as a martyr, and miracles were claimed at his shrine. St. Edmund (841–69) was another East-Anglian king. Defeated in battle by Vikings, he refused to renounce his faith and rule as his victor's vassal, so was put to death. St. Edward the Confessor (1003–66) was admired for his care for the poor, his accessibility to his subjects, and his contribution to the founding of Westminster Abbey, where he is buried. He was regarded as the main patron saint of England until this place was taken by St. George.

right: **Richard II and his Patron Saints, Wilton Diptych, 1395–9, English or French**
His patrons are SS. John the Baptist, Edward, and Edmund.
next page: **St. Augustine Preaching to the Saxons, Stephen B. Carlill, reproduced in *The Pageant of British History*, 1909, English**
Augustine preaches to Ethelbert, King of Kent, and Queen Bertha.

Saint Wenceslas

The saint that the English-speaking world remembers in the popular Christmas carol "Good King Wenceslas" was not a king, but a duke, and the story told in those verses is a delightful fiction. The real St. Wenceslas (907–29?) ruled Bohemia according to the Christian principles he had been taught by his grandmother, St. Ludmilla (860–921). He looked to the Western church for inspiration, and placed his duchy under the protection of Germany, welcoming German priests and favoring the Latin over the old Slavic liturgy. His attempt to modernize and Christianize his homeland made him political as well as religious enemies, including his own brother, Boleslaw, who was implicated in Wenceslas' murder in 929.

Three years later, Boleslaw, regretting his part in the crime, had Wenceslas' body transferred to the St. Vitus church in Prague, where it was visited by an increasing number of pilgrims. By 985 St. Wenceslas' feast day was being celebrated, and by the year 1000 or so he was acknowledged as the patron saint of Bohemia. His crown became the symbol of Czech nationalism, and a fine equestrian statue of him now dominates the square named after him in Prague.

right: King Wenceslas, Anne Anderson in *Old English Nursery Songs*, undated, English
The real saint was known for his many virtues, but the incident described in the Good King Wenceslas carol is fictional.

Good King Wenceslas looked out on the feast of Stephen,
When the snow lay round about, deep and crisp and even;
Brightly shone the moon that night, tho' the frost was cruel,
When a poor man came in sight gath'ring winter fuel.

"Hither, page, and stand by me, if thou know'st it, telling,
Yonder peasant, who is he? Where and what his dwelling?"
"Sire, he lives a good league hence, underneath the mountain;
Right against the forest fence, by Saint Agnes' fountain."

"Bring me flesh, and bring me wine, bring me pine logs hither:
Thou and I will see him dine, when we bear them thither."
Page and monarch, forth they went, forth they went together;
Through the rude wind's wild lament and the bitter weather.

"Sire, the night is darker now, and the wind blows stronger;
Fails my heart, I know not how, I can go no longer."
"Mark my footsteps, my good page. Tread thou in them boldly:
Thou shalt find the winter's rage freeze thy blood less coldly."

In his master's steps he trod, where the snow lay dinted;
Heat was in the very sod which the saint had printed.
Therefore, Christian men, be sure, wealth or rank possessing,
Ye who now will bless the poor, shall yourselves find blessing.

CHRISTMAS CAROL, J. M. NEALE, 1854

St. Vladimir and St. Stephen

The Russian ruler St. Vladimir (955–1015) was a violent and enthusiastic pagan until his conversion to Christianity in 989. After marrying the daughter of the emperor Basil II, he encouraged Greek missionaries to bring the gospel to his people. He ordered pagan idols pulled down and established churches and monasteries in their place. He was known for his generosity to the poor, but also for his harshness to those who resisted his efforts to Christianize his country.

St. Stephen of Hungary (c. 975–1038) was the first king of his country, which was Christianized and united under his rule. His right hand is treasured as his nation's most sacred relic.

... raise thine eyes and see the honors that the Lord has laid up for you in heaven and the fame that He has given you among your children. Look also on the city, shining with glory, the flourishing churches, the progress of Christianity, look on this city, sanctified by the holy icons, radiant and fragrant with incense, resounding with praise and hymns to God.

METROPOLITAN HILARION INVOKING KING VLADIMIR

Saintly Queens

St. Margaret of Scotland (1046–93) was married to King Malcolm III, by whom she had eight children. She founded monasteries and churches, and restored the abbey of Iona. She gave freely to the poor, ransomed prisoners, and was intensely prayerful in her private life.

St. Elizabeth of Hungary (1207–31) was generous to the poorest of her subjects, founding hospitals and providing for orphans. She had three children by her husband, Louis IV of Thuringia. Brokenhearted by his death in the Crusades in 1227, she became a third order Franciscan (a lay follower of St Francis) and devoted her life to prayer and to caring for the poor with her own hands. She died three years later and was canonized by Pope Gregory IX in 1235. One of her distant relatives was St. Elizabeth of Portugal (1271–1336). She too, was a queen and a mother who founded hospitals and orphanages. After her husband's death in 1324, she retired to a life of poverty and prayer. She was canonized by Urban VIII in 1626.

right: Madonna and Child with Donors, Lippo Vanni, 1341–1375, Italian Detail showing St. Elizabeth of Hungary.

Scandinavian Royal Saints

The patron saint of Norway is Olaf (995–1030), who had been a warrior and a pirate before his conversion to Christianity. Having established himself as king, he set about Christianizing his country, but rebels drove him into exile and he was killed in a battle fought to regain his throne.

St. Eric (d. 1160) was the king of Sweden who consolidated Christianity in his own country, and who was assassinated on the site of the present cathedral of Uppsala. St. Canute, king of Denmark (d. 1086) was killed as he knelt at the altar of the church of St. Alban at Odonsee.

... miracles began to be manifested at St. Olaf's body: a light was seen over it at night; a blind man recovered his sight on pressing his fingers, dipped in the saint's blood, to his eyes; springs of water with healing properties flowed from his grave ...

HEINSKRINGLA *THE SAGA OF ST. OLAF*

left: **Manuscript reproduced in O. A. Overland, *Norges Historie*, 1887–93, Norwegian**
Olaf II Haraldsson, also known as St. Olaf, King of Norway.

King Louis IX of France

King Louis IX of France (1214–70) embodied the highest ideals of medieval monarchy, and was canonized by Boniface VIII in 1297. Austere and prayerful, he had a reputation for honesty and fairness in his political dealings, though these were not always successful in human terms. Nor were the two crusades he undertook, which both ended in disaster. St. Louis' spiritual enterprises, however, had better outcomes. He founded the monasteries of Vauvert, Maubuisson, and Royaumont, and a 300–bed hospital for the poor and blind. He was admired for his impartiality and respect for justice.

Dear son, if you come to reign, do that which befits a king, that is, be so just as to deviate in nothing from justice, whatever may befall you.

ST. LOUIS IX OF FRANCE

right: **Louis IX with John the Baptist, attrib. Van Eyck, reproduced in *Chroniqueurs de l'Histoire de France*, 1883–6, French**
The king-saint was a model ruler of great personal piety.

Above all things: forget not the poor, but support them to the extent of your means. Give to the orphan, protect the widow, and permit the mighty to destroy no man. Take not the life of the just or the unjust, nor permit him to be killed. Destroy no Christian soul, even though he be guilty of murder.

SAINT VLADIMIR, AS QUOTED IN *THE CHRONICLE OF NESTOR*

First of all, with the help of God, she made the King himself most attentive to works of justice, mercy, almsgiving, and other virtues... Since he clearly perceived that Christ was truly dwelling in her heart, he hastened all the more quickly to obey her wishes and prudent counsels. What she refused, he refused; and what she loved, he loved for the love of her love.

TURGOT, *LIFE OF ST. MARGARET, QUEEN OF SCOTLAND*

Make the strangers welcome in this land,
let them keep their languages and customs,
for weak and fragile is the realm which is based
on a single language or on a single set of customs

ST. STEPHEN OF HUNGARY

Weep not, I shall not die; and as I
leave the land of the dying, I trust to
see the blessings of the Lord in the
land of the living.

ST. EDWARD THE CONFESSOR

Edmund the blessed, king of the East Angles, was wise
and honorable and by his excellent conduct ever glorified
Almighty God. He was humble and devout, and continued
so steadfast that he would not yield to shameful sins, nor
in any direction did he bend aside his practices, but was
always mindful of true doctrine.

AELFRIC, *THE PASSION OF ST. EDMUND, KING AND MARTYR*

St. Joan of Arc

The worlds of kings and commoners meet in the story of St. Joan of Arc (1412–31), one of the most popular saints of all time. An illiterate shepherdess who saw life with childlike simplicity, from the age of fourteen Joan had mystical experiences in which she heard the voices of the Archangel Michael and of St. Catherine and St. Margaret. Joan believed that they told her to go to the aid of the Dauphin, the crown prince of France, whose throne was then threatened by the English. She did what her voices asked. Joan was so confident and obviously sincere that she was eventually granted an audience with the Dauphin. He attempted to reveal her as a fraud by setting an impersonator in his throne, but she picked the real Dauphin out of the crowd, knelt before him, and revealed to him a secret that persuaded him that she was indeed sent by God.

In a suit of white armor and carrying a banner bearing the words "Jesus and Mary," Joan led the French troops to victory at Orleans, turning the tide of the Hundred Years War, and paving the way for the Dauphin to be crowned (as Charles VII) in Reims cathedral in July 1429. She stood beside him during the coronation service. And then things started to go wrong. The campaign stalled and though she relieved Compiègne, it was then besieged by the Burgundians, who were allies of the English.

left: **Joan of Arc, Robert Alexander Hillingford, 1825–1904, English**
St. Joan is one of the patron saints of France.

Joan was finally captured, and Charles left her to her fate. The Burgundians sold her to the English, who had her tried for heresy and witchcraft by a church court presided over by the bishop of Beauvais.

Much was made of her decision to wear male dress. She saw it as a way of protecting her innocence when surrounded by soldiery; it became even more important to her when she was at the mercy of the men who kept her prisoner. The church represented it as a sin against nature, and condemned her claim to have heard saintly voices as heresy. Exhausted and threatened with torture, she put her name to a recantation, but almost immediately withdrew it. She was declared a heretic and handed over to the secular authorities for punishment. She was burned at the stake in Rouen in 1431. In front of the pyre was a board upon which were painted words that the illiterate, nineteen-year-old peasant girl could not have understood: "Jehanne who calls herself La Pucelle, liar, pernicious deceiver of the people, sorceress, superstitious blasphemer of God, presumptuous disbeliever in the faith of Jesus Christ, boastful, idolatrous, cruel, dissolute invoker of devils, apostate, schismatic and heretic." In 1456 a church commission reexamined Joan's case and quashed the verdict; she was canonized by Pope Benedict XV in 1920, nearly 500 years after her death.

Asked if she knew whether she were in the grace of God, she answered: "If I am not, may God put me there; if I am, may He keep me there."

TRANSCRIPT OF THE TRIAL OF JOAN OF ARC

The story of an innocent young woman used, discarded, and condemned as a spiritual seductress by cynical men of the world has fired the imagination of artists of all disciplines. Mark Twain believed that "she was perhaps the only entirely unselfish person whose name has a place in profane history" and considered his historical novel *The Personal Recollections of Joan of Arc* (1896) the best book he had ever written. George Bernard Shaw turned Joan into a powerful mouthpiece for his own opinions in his stage play St. Joan of 1924, characterizing her as a proto-Protestant "crushed between those mighty forces, the Church and the Law." The work won him the 1925 Nobel Prize for Literature, though he refused to accept it. Vita Sackville-West's *St. Joan of Arc* (1936) is a both a historical biography and a work of high art. Jean Anouilh's 1953 play *L'Alouette* ("The Lark") presents her as a "phenomenon" like that "of a daisy or of the sky or of a bird."

St. Thérèse of Lisieux (1873–97) wrote a play about Joan that was performed in her Carmelite convent. She played the leading part herself. Statues and paintings of St. Joan abound in France, which adopted her as a national patron. Few French churches or chapels are without one. There and elsewhere, she has become an instantly recognizable icon that expresses courage, patriotism, and femininity— either as the martyr at the stake, or the warrior-saint triumphant. .

next page: **Joan of Arc Led to her Execution, Isidore Patrois, 1815–84, French**
After Joan's execution, her ashes were thrown into the river Seine.

Joan—a Saint for the Cinema

More movies have been made about St. Joan than about any other saint. One of the first was Georges Hatot's *Jeanne d'Arc* (1898). At least four more were made before 1917, when she was the subject of Cecil B. DeMille's first historical spectacle, *Joan the Woman*. DeMille invented a romantic relationship between Joan and one of her comrades-in-arms, Gilles de Rais, which was doubly inappropriate, for the real Joan's devotion to her virginity was unassailable, and the real Gilles de Rais' sexual interests lay in raping and murdering children. (He was executed for his crimes in 1440.)

Most film critics agree that the Danish director Carl Theodor Dreyer's *La Passion de Jeanne d'Arc* (1928) is the greatest movie ever made about St. Joan, and some judge it the greatest movie of all time. It shows none of Joan's glories or military triumphs, but deals only with her trial and execution, which are distilled into a film of extraordinary pathos. Dreyer uses angled close-ups of the faces of the saint and her tormentors to emphasize her suffering and their cruelty. Belittled and bullied, she is presented as an innocent with an honesty that her interrogators refuse to comprehend. It is harrowing to watch, and was harrowing to make. The actress who played the heroine, Maria Falconetti, wept real tears and displayed genuine grief; one of the film crew later described how they felt they were not making a film, but "living Joan's drama, and we often wanted to intervene and save her."

right: Jean Seberg as Joan of Arc in Otto Preminger's *St. Joan*, 1957
Jean Seberg is shown in full battle dress as the French heroine, St. Joan of Arc in the film version of George Bernard Shaw's *Saint Joan*.

Marc de Gastyne's film *La Merveilleuse Vie de Jeanne d'Arc* was also made in 1928, and Gustav Ucicky's *Das Mädchen Johanna* was released in 1935. Victor Fleming's *Joan of Arc* of 1948 starred Ingrid Bergman, who was fascinated by Joan's character, though she perhaps does not convey her spirituality convincingly. The film is spectacular, but is not a deep study of the saint.

Roberto Rosselini's *Giovanna d'Arco al Rogo* (1954) was based on Paul Claudel and Arthur Honegger's intense, psychological oratorio *Jeanne d'Arc au Bûcher* of 1938. (Both titles amount to "Joan of Arc at the Stake.") The year 1954 also saw the production of Jean Delannoy's *Destinées*, three stories of war and womanhood, one of which is called *Jeanne*.

Otto Preminger's 1957 *Saint Joan* has a script by Graham Greene that is based on the play by George Bernard Shaw. Preminger chose the seventeen-year-old unknown actress Jean Seberg to play the lead. It made her career, but she did not make a convincing St. Joan, even though she was accidentally burned by the special-effect flames during her "execution."

Florence Carrez stars in Robert Bresson's *Le Procès de Jeanne d'Arc* (1962), which is closely based on the transcript of Joan's trials. The film is admired for the unsensational simplicity of its technique, which allows the moving facts of the story to speak for themselves. Sandrine Bonnaire plays Joan as a fanatical freedom-fighter in Jacques Rivette's *Jeanne La Pucelle* (1993), and makes Joan more of a rebel than a saint.

Luc Bresson's *The Messenger: The Story of Joan of Arc* (1999) is a work of imaginative fiction that departs in many ways from the traditional story of the saint.

Taking into account ... all the circumstances—her origin, youth, sex, illiteracy, early environment, and the obstructing conditions under which she exploited her high gifts and made her conquests in the field and before the courts that tried her for her life—she is easily and by far the most extraordinary person the human race has ever produced.

MARK TWAIN, *THE PERSONAL RECOLLECTIONS OF JOAN OF ARC*

chapter 8

Sacrifice and Martyrdom

Facing Death with Courage

Christians have always recognized their martyrs as saints, because their willingness to die for their faith demonstrates a love for God that is absolute. The word "martyr" means "witness," and a martyr's death witnesses to God's promise of eternal life. The first Christians called the anniversaries of their saints' martyrdoms *natales*, for they were seen as heavenly birthdays rather than earthly deaths.

The early saints embraced death not merely with courage, but with enthusiasm. Some actively sought it. Tertullian and Eusebius describe believers handing themselves in to the Roman authorities during times of persecution, knowing that the punishment for adhering to Christianity was death. The heroism of such martyrs was applauded, but they were not held up as examples to be followed. Contriving one's own martyrdom was seen as unorthodox. It was also condemned as unwise. The second-century *Encyclical Epistle of the Church at Smyrna, Concerning the Martyrdom of St. Polycarp* cites Quintus, a Phrygian, who persuaded a number of fellow-Christians to join him and surrender themselves for trial. His companions faced death with courage, but when Quintus saw the wild beasts waiting to tear him to pieces, he apostatized. The letter warns against actively seeking death as a martyr, for "the Gospel does not teach so to do."

previous page: **Nuns Praying Before Martyrs and Saints, c. 1543, unknown artist**
Martyrs have always been regarded as powerful examples and intercessors.
left: **The Martyrdom of St. Florian, Albrecht Altdorfer, c. 1530, German**
The martyr was thrown into the river Enns.

St. Stephen

The first martyr of the Christian church was St. Stephen, whose story is told in the Acts of the Apostles. When the apostles asked the Christian community to name seven men who would help them to look after the poor, their first choice was Stephen, who is described as "a man full of faith and of the Holy Spirit," who "did great wonders and miracles among the people."

His preaching made enemies as well as converts. His message was that the Messiah who the Jews were waiting for had already come: it was Jesus, and they had rejected him. Stephen's opponents argued with him publicly, but he knew his scripture well, and got the better of them. They resented this challenge to their authority, and spread it about that he had blasphemed against God and Moses. He was dragged before the Jewish court, the Sanhedrin, and false witnesses were produced to testify against him.

When the High Priest asked him if the charges were true, he replied by preaching a long sermon on how their common ancestors had rejected and persecuted God's prophets, including Moses. His listeners were outraged. They rose up as a mob, dragged him outside, and stoned him to death. As they were stoning him, he was heard to say "Lord Jesus, receive my spirit" and then, in a loud voice, "Lord, lay not this sin to their charge." One of those in the crowd who saw him die was Saul, who was later to become St. Paul.

right: **St. Stephen the Martyr, Francesco Francia, 1450–1517, Italian**
St. Stephen was one of the first deacons of the church.

The Cordoban Martyrs

Although contriving one's martyrdom was seen as unorthodox, it does not, of course, mean that a Christian is always forbidden to take active steps that will or might lead to death. In ninth-century Spain, an outburst of apostolic enthusiasm in Cordoba led to forty-eight martyrdoms including that of St. Eulogius (d. 859), who recorded the events of the decade in his *Memorial of the Saints*. This makes it clear that the Christians could have survived by keeping their heads down— which is what their bishop, Reccafredus, wanted them to do—but that some of them chose to assert the truths of their faith and their right to proselytize. The Moors who had conquered Spain 150 years earlier tolerated Christianity as long as it did not challenge their authority. They allowed Christians to live in peace, provided they did not attempt to convert Muslims to their religion.

The martyrs of Cordoba did just that. Eulogius was beheaded on March 11th 859 for helping to hide a young Muslim convert to Christianity. He was elected archbishop of Toledo, but did not live long enough to be consecrated. His relics are now in Oviedo cathedral.

right: **The Vision of Eulogius, mid-16th century, Russian**
The martyrs of Cordoba refused to compromise with their non-Christian rulers.

St. John Fisher

Complicated choices were demanded of the martyrs of the Reformation, when Christian duties of political and religious obedience were intertwined. The question asked of Englishmen in the 1530s was not "Will you renounce Christianity?" but "Will you swear on oath that the king is head of the church?" The wrong answer brought execution, and almost everybody said "yes," including the bishops—with the single exception of St. John Fisher (1469–1535), bishop of Rochester.

Fisher had fiercely defended the validity of Henry VIII's marriage to Catharine of Aragon, which the king wanted annulled so that he could marry Anne Boleyn. In 1531 the bishop further enraged the monarch by acknowledging him Supreme Head of the Church of England only "so far as the law of Christ allows." The 1534 Act of Treasons made it a capital offense to "maliciously wish, will, or desire by words or writing, or by craft imagine, practice or attempt" to deny the sovereign, his queen, or heirs any of their titles. Even to think that the king was not head of the English church was defined as treasonable; to express that thought was evidence of the crime. Fisher was imprisoned in the Tower of London for ten months, during which time his health, already weakened by his personal austerities, deteriorated severely. When his gown was stripped from him at his execution, witnesses were shocked to see "a long, lean, slender body, nothing in manner but skin and bare bones… the flesh clean wasted away and a very image of death, and, as one might say, death in a man's shape, and using a man's voice."

right: **The Martyr and Prelate John Fisher, unnamed engraving**
The saint was a great preacher and patron of learning.

St. Thomas More

The dilemma that English Catholics faced during the Reformation was neatly summed up by St. Thomas More (1478–1535) at his execution, when he announced that he died "the king's good servant, but God's first." Thomas had enjoyed a comfortable upbringing as the eldest son of Sir John More, a well-regarded lawyer who served as a judge in the King's Bench court. He became a page in the service of John Morton, the Archbishop of Canterbury, who declared that the young Thomas would become a "marvellous man."

Thou wilt give me this day a greater benefit than ever any mortal man can be able to give me. Pluck up thy spirits, man, and be not afraid to do thine office.

ST. THOMAS MORE'S WORDS TO HIS EXECUTIONER

left: **Sir Thomas More, Hans Holbein the Younger, 1527, German**
St. Thomas More was condemned to be hanged, drawn and quartered, but the sentence was commuted to beheading.

More's talent as a lawyer, his reputation for wider learning, and his personal integrity had led Henry VIII (1491–1547) to single him out for royal preferment. In 1529 he awarded him the Lord Chancellorship, the highest political post in the land. More was the first layman to hold it. The king also cultivated him as a friend, for Sir Thomas' cheerfulness, tact, and kindness made him a highly attractive personality.

In 1519 the Dutch humanist scholar Desiderius Erasmus (c. 1466–1536) had written of him: "He seems born and framed for friendship, and is a most faithful and enduring friend. He is easy of access to all; but if he chances to become familiar with one whose vices admit no correction, he manages to loosen and let go the intimacy rather than to break it off suddenly."

He was not able to disengage himself so gracefully from the king. Shortly after More's appointment as Chancellor, Henry issued a proclamation ordering the clergy to swear an oath acknowledging the king to be "Supreme Head" of the Church. The king's determination to reject the authority of the pope and to divorce Catherine of Aragon made More's position increasingly untenable. Unable to support these policies, and knowing that to contradict them publicly would lead to dismissal and death, he resigned the Chancellorship in 1532. He retired to the country, where he hoped to be left in peace. But his reputation was too great for him to be allowed just to slip away. His silence was felt to be as damaging as active disloyalty; the king wanted either his approval or his head.

The Act of Succession of 1534 made More's silence treasonable. It required anyone who was asked, to take an oath accepting the issue of Henry and his new queen, Anne Boleyn, as legitimate heirs to the throne, and repudiating "any foreign authority, prince or potentate"—a reference to the spiritual authority of the pope. When More was ordered to take the oath, he refused, and was imprisoned and charged with treason. When questioned, he refused to comment on the royal marriage or on parliament's authority to make the king the head of the church, knowing that his answers would be used as evidence of treasonable intent.

Only at the trial itself, when false evidence of his spoken opinion was produced, did he declare his outright and absolute objection. The death sentence was inevitable. More faced his execution with exemplary confidence. When he put his head upon the block, he joked with his executioner, asking for enough time to move his beard out of the way, for that part of him "had never offended his Highness." St. Thomas More was canonized by Pope Pius XI in 1935.

Farewell, my dear child, and pray for me, and I shall for you and all your friends, that we may merrily meet in heaven.

FROM THOMAS MORE'S LAST LETTER TO HIS DAUGHTER, MARGARET, WRITTEN ON THE EVE OF HIS EXECUTION

The Forty Martyrs

In 1970, Pope Paul VI canonized forty English and Welsh saints martyred under anti-Catholic laws between 1535 and 1679. Among them were the Jesuit priest St. Edmund Campion (1540–81), and St. Nicholas Owen (c. 1550–1606), a Jesuit lay brother. Campion was a brilliant scholar who wrote defenses of Catholicism. Owen, once a carpenter, had constructed secret "priests' holes" in houses all over the country. He revealed nothing to his torturers, who racked him so severely that his entrails burst from his body and he died in agony.

One of the layfolk among the Forty Martyrs was St. John Rigby (c. 1570–1600), a servant sent to court to explain that his master's daughter could not attend because she was ill. Questioned about his religion, he declared himself a Catholic and refused to save himself by promising to conform. When the executioners seized him he cried "God forgive you!"; they stood on his throat to shut him up. When they were pulling out his heart, he had enough strength left to throw them off before they could finish their work. A different sort of cruelty was visited upon St. Margaret Clitherow (1556–86). Charged with harboring priests, she refused to plead, thus saving her friends and family from having to give evidence against her and implicating themselves. It took fifteen minutes for her to die crushed by heavy weights.

right: **St. Edmund Campion, undated and unnamed engraving**
St. Edmund Campion worked as an underground priest until his capture.
next page: **Pressing Margaret Clitherow to Death, undated and unnamed engraving**
The saint hid Catholic priests in her house—a capital offense.

When she felt the kill-weights crush
She told His name times-over three;
I suffer this, she said, for Thee.

GERARD MANLEY HOPKINS, *MARGARET CLITHEROE*

You thought perhaps when lerned Campion dyes,
His pen must cease, his sugred tong be still,
But you forgot how lowde his death it cries,
How farre beyond the sound of tongue and quil,
You did not know how rare and great a good
It was to write his precious giftes in blood.

ST. HENRY WALPOLE (ATTRIB.) *UPON THE DEATH OF M. EDMUND CAMPION,*

May I be received among the
martyrs in your presence today as a
rich and pleasing sacrifice.

ST. POLYCARP

Then shall they deliver you up to be afflicted, and shall kill you: and ye shall be hated of all nations for my name's sake.

MATTHEW 24:9

... ye shall be drawn ... upon hurdles to the place of execution, and there be hanged and let down alive, and your privy parts cut off, and your entrails taken out and burned in your sight; then your heads to be cut off and your bodies divided into four parts, to be disposed of at her Majesty's pleasure.

SENTENCE PASSED UPON ST. EDMUND CAMPION AND COMPANIONS, 1581

St. Jean de Brébeuf

Martyrdoms took place in the New World, too. St. Jean de Brébeuf (1593–1649), the French Jesuit who brought the gospel to the Huron Indians of Canada suffered a violent death far from his place of birth. He had paddled a canoe 800 miles (1300 km.) to reach the Huron Indians, and studied their language and customs so that he could express the truths of Christianity through their own culture. In 1649 he was captured in a raid by the Huron's enemies, the Iroquois. They tied him to a stake and tortured him for hours. Having scalded him with boiling water in a mockery of baptism, they hung red-hot axes around his neck, scalped him, and thrust a red-hot iron down his throat before cutting his heart out. Witnesses state that he endured all this in absolute silence. St. Jean de Brébeuf was canonized by Pope Pius XI in 1930.

Within a lodge of broken bark the tender babe was found
A ragged robe of rabbit skin enwrapped his beauty round;
And as the hunter braves drew nigh,
The angel song rang loud and high:
Jesus your King is born, Jesus is born,
In excelsis gloria!

HURON CHRISTMAS CAROL OF ST. JEAN DE BRÉBEUF

right: **St. Jean de Brébeuf Challenging the Indian Council,**
undated and unnamed engraving
Saint Jean de Brébeuf (1593–1649), was a Jesuit missionary who was sent to try to convert the Native Americans.

I. Silvestre ex.
Illot. sc.   cum privil. Regis.

Martyrs in Japan

Many saints became martyrs in the missions that took Christianity to parts of the world that were unknown or unreachable in the days of Christ. In 1549, the gospel was brought to Japan by the Jesuit St. Francis Xavier (1506–52). He was not martyred for his efforts—he died three years later from exhaustion—and the Christian community he founded was tolerated by the government. But in 1587 Christianity was proscribed because of fears that the missionaries were the spearhead of a European attempt to conquer the country politically. In 1597 Emperor Toyotomi Hideyoshi (1536–98) executed twenty-six Christians near Nagasaki. The group included St. Paul Miki, a Japanese aristocrat who had become a Jesuit priest, several foreign Franciscans, and sixteen laymen. All were canonized in 1862.

Five further waves of persecution led to the near-eradication of the visible Christian community in Japan by 1640, with many thousands dying for their faith. The victims of Emperor Tokugawa Yemitsu's purge of 1637 included the Filipino St. Lorenzo Ruiz, who had taken a boat to Japan to avoid legal problems at home. He found even more serious ones on arrival. He was arrested and was asked if he was a Christian, then a capital offense. He said he was, but then asked whether he would be spared if he recanted. Before the answer came, he reaffirmed his faith and was cruelly tortured and beheaded.

left: **The Japanese Martyrs, Jacques Callot,**
17th-century engraving, French
Twenty-three Franciscans are crucified at Mongasaki by order of the emperor Taicosam; angels in the skies above prepare to welcome the martyrs to Paradise.

I have committed no crime, and the only reason why I am put to death is that I have been teaching the doctrine of Our Lord Jesus Christ. I am very happy to die for such a cause, and see my death as a great blessing from the Lord. At this critical time, when, you can rest assured that I will not try to deceive you, I want to stress and make it unmistakably clear that man can find no way to salvation other than the Christian way.

PAUL MIKI, JAPANESE CONVERT

The Christian must be consumed with the infinite beauty of holiness and the infinite damnability of sin.

THOMAS CARLYLE, COMMEMORATION OF MARTYRS OF JAPAN, 1597

I know thy works, and where thou dwellest, even where Satan's seat is: and thou holdest fast my name, and hast not denied my faith, even in those days wherein An'tipas was my faithful martyr, who was slain among you, where Satan dwelleth.

REVELATIONS 2: 13

The Ugandan Martyrs

The "Martyrs of Uganda," St. Charles Lwanga and Companions, were killed between 1885 and 1887 on the orders of the ruling *kabaka* of Buganda, Mwanga II, who saw his political authority threatened by the presence of European missionaries. Christianity was received with great enthusiasm by the converts, but it also placed them at odds with mainstream religious customs in Uganda.

As a young prince, Mwanga had demonstrated no hostility to the missionaries. However, his attitude changed dramatically when he became king. The once friendly young prince who had behaved with a benevolent attitude turned into a violent persecutor of Christians and all foreigners.

Mwanga was not only intolerant of the missionaries' religious beliefs, he was also also outraged that converts to Christianity challenged his right to use his servants for his sexual pleasure. Charles Lwanga was the courtier responsible for the royal pageboys, and when he rebuked the *kabaka* for assaulting them, Mwanga had him executed.

Lwanga was slowly burned to death. Mwanga then assembled the pages and ordered the Christians among them to step forward. Fifteen did so. Invited to renounce their faith, they refused; they were wrapped in mats of reeds and burned alive. The Ugandan martyrs were canonized by Pope Paul VI in 1964.

A Christian who gives his life for God is not afraid to die.

JOSEPH MUKASA BALIKUDDEMBE, UGANDAN MARTYR

I lift mine eyes, and all the windows blaze
With forms of saints and holy men who died,
Here martyred and hereafter glorified

HENRY WADSWORTH LONGFELLOW, *DIVINA COMMEDIA*

Blessed are ye, when men shall revile you, and persecute you, and shall say all manner of evil against you falsely, for my sake.

MATTHEW 5, 11

Revolutionary Martyrs

Just as King Henry VIII of England had imposed an oath that led to martyrdom, so did the regime of revolutionary France. In 1790, all French bishops and clergy were required to swear to uphold a law that effectively denied the pope authority in France. In 1792, many of those that had refused were rounded up, along with other enemies of the state, and herded into several buildings in Paris.

Among them was the archbishop of Arles, Blessed Jean du Lau. In September, armed bands visited each location and hacked the prisoners to death. Similar scenes were enacted in other parts of the country, and many more suffered or died during the attempt to dechristianize France. Pope St. Pius X beatified sixteen martyrs of the French Revolution in 1906. Pope Pius XI beatified 191 others in 1926. Sixty-four more were beatified by Pope John Paul II in 1995.

The first group to be beatified were the martyrs of Compiègne, a community of Carmelite nuns whose sacrifice inspired Gertrud von le Fort to write the novel *The Song at the Scaffold* upon which the composer François Poulenc based his opera *Dialogues des Carmélites*. Many French revolutionaries saw the very existence of a contemplative religious order as an affront to their tyrannical notion of "Liberty."

In 1790 and 1791 the taking of vows and the wearing of religious habits were forbidden. Seeing what was coming, the nuns of Compiègne made a communal act of consecration in which they offered their lives to God for the sake of peace. In 1792 their convent was locked, and the sisters were dispersed. For two years, they met secretly for prayer, but in 1794 they were arrested and tried for offenses against the state. The verdict was never in doubt, and the nuns and two lay servants were guillotined on July 17th 1794. Before their execution they knelt down together, sang the *Veni Creator* and renewed aloud their baptismal and religious vows. Ten days later, the Reign of Terror was over.

I learned from a person who was a witness to their martyrdom that the youngest of these good Carmelites was called first and that she went to kneel before her venerable Superior, asked her blessing and permission to die. She then mounted the scaffold singing *Laudate Dominum omnes gentes*. She then went to place herself beneath the blade without allowing the executioner to touch her. All the others did the same. The Venerable Mother was the last sacrificed. During the whole time, there was not a single drum-roll; but there reigned a profound silence.

LETTER OF MOTHER ÉMILIENNE, SUPERIOR GENERAL OF
THE SISTERS OF CHARITY OF NEVERS

Revolutionary anti-clerical fervor also led to persecutions of the church in Mexico—twenty-five of the many souls who were martyred there between 1915 and 1937 were canonized by Pope John Paul II in 2000. Perhaps the most dramatic example of the choice facing the priests whose activities were outlawed was that presented to St. Rodrigo Aguilar in 1927. Captured by government troops, he was taken to the main square of Ejutla to be hanged. When the noose was put around his neck, he was told he would be spared if he would only say, "Long live the supreme government!" Instead, he called out "Long live Christ the King and Our Lady of Guadalupe!" He was hauled up and half-hanged, then asked again; he offered the same reply and was once more strangled near to death. The third time he was left hanging until he died.

The martyrdom of Blessed Miguel Pro (1891–1927) caused international outrage, because his show trial on trumped-up charges of political terrorism was followed by an execution to which the Mexican president Plutarco Calles invited the press. The move backfired: the photographs that were taken included one of the moment of his death, in which the martyr holds his arms wide, making a cross. Their publication proved so counterproductive that the government attempted to recall them, and then made possession of them a crime.

The martyrdom of St. Toribio Romo was less public, and showed a different kind of heroism. Knowing the risks of exercising his ministry, he told his sister, "I am cowardly, so if one day God wants me to be killed, I hope he will give me a rapid death, with only the time necessary to pray for my enemies." In the early hours of February 25th, 1928, government troops broke into the abandoned factory where Fr Toribio had been saying mass for the local people, and shot him in his bed. They then stripped his corpse and displayed it on the steps of the town hall.

During the Spanish Civil War (1936–39) and the period that immediately preceded it, nearly 7,000 priests, monks, and nuns, thirteen bishops and countless Catholic laymen and laywomen were martyred for their faith. To date, ten have been canonized and over 500 beatified. The event was not a war of religion, but a contest for control between the forces of conservatism and ultraconservatism that rallied around the Nationalists, and the Republican liberal-socialist alliance. The latter included atheistic communists who saw the church as a mortal enemy that had to be crushed. In areas that fell into Republican control, they formed themselves into militias that murdered priests and nuns on sight, or set up Soviet-style courts that sentenced them to death.

One of the first female martyrs was the 27-year-old Carmelite nun Blessed Teresa del Niño Jesús y de San Juan de la Cruz, who was captured and executed in 1936. Her captors offered to spare her if she called out "Viva el Comunismo!" She cried "Viva Cristo Rey!" and they shot her. When 75-year-old Blessed Ceferino Jiménez Malla (1861–1936) was arrested for sheltering a priest, he was offered freedom if he would deny his faith and throw away his rosary. He refused and was shot by a firing squad. He was beatified in 1997.

Countless Christians were martyred under the atheistic Communist regimes of China and the former Soviet Union—and twenty-six Ukrainian martyrs were beatified by Pope John Paul II in 2001. Blessed Joachim Senkivskyi, the much-loved abbot of Drohobych, was boiled to death in a cauldron by Bolsheviks in the town's prison on 29th June 1941.

next page: **Chromolithograph after Charles Louis Lucien Müller, 19th century, French**
A group of Christians meet in secrecy to hear mass during the French Revolution.

St. Maximilian Kolbe

The Polish St. Maximilian Kolbe spent his whole life in the service of God, but it is for the extraordinary generosity of his death that he is most remembered. After joining the Franciscans in 1910, he founded friaries in Poland, Japan, and India. When Germany invaded Poland in 1939, he returned to the friary that he had established near Warsaw, and turned it into a haven for 3,000 refugees, of whom two-thirds were Jews. In May 1941 the Nazi occupiers closed the friary and sent Maximilian and four of his Franciscan co-workers to the death camp of Auschwitz.

In July a man from Kolbe's hut went missing, and according to camp rules, ten men were selected for execution in reprisal. One of them was Franciszek Gajowniczek, who had been imprisoned for helping the Polish Resistance. When he was picked, he cried out, "My poor wife! My poor children! What will they do?" Kolbe offered to take his place and he and nine others were locked in a cellar and left to starve. Kolbe comforted his fellow-prisoners while their strength lasted. After a fortnight, he was the only one still alive, and he was executed by an injection of carbolic acid. Maximilian Kolbe was canonized by Pope John Paul II in 1982. The man whose place he took lived until 1995.

Beyond armies of occupation and the hecatombs of extermination camps, there are two irreconcilable enemies in the depth of every soul: good and evil, sin and love.

ST. MAXIMILIAN KOLBE

left: **Photograph of St. Maximilian Kolbe, c. 1940, Poland**
St. Maximilian Kolbe is known as a "martyr of charity."

I wish to die for that man. I am old; he has a wife and children.

ST. MAXIMILIAN KOLBE

The souls of the Saints, who followed the footsteps of Christ, rejoice in Heaven: and because they shed their blood for His love, therefore do they exult with Christ, world without end.

ROMAN MISSAL

The noble army of martyrs praise thee.

NICETAS OF REMESIANA, *TE DEUM LAUDAMUS*

Who falls for love of God shall rise
a star.

BEN JONSON

If anything happens in your life contrary to
your prayers, you should give thanks to
God, knowing that his will is far superior to
your own. Through thanking God in all
circumstances, you will learn to conform
your will to his.

ST. AUGUSTINE OF HIPPO

He that findeth his life shall lose it:
and he that loseth his life for my
sake shall find it.

MATTHEW, 10:39

Interview with Neville Kyrke-Smith

National Director of Aid to the Church in Need UK

Your work takes you to places where Christians were persecuted under atheistic communism. What do you know of the martyrs of this period?

It is quite stunning that hardly any books or articles have been written on martyrs under communism. Perhaps this is due to a sympathetic 1960s Marxist hangover in the West, or the fact that many former communist countries have the old guard ruling, even if wearing different dictatorial hats. There is also an unwillingness of people to admit their knowledge, or even involvement in the incredible sufferings that took place. For example, no one will ever know the actual number of those who died in the gulag prison camps or in enforced exile in the Soviet Union last century. Many of the camps have now been destroyed, but it is estimated that perhaps between 20 to 30 million died—hundreds of thousands of whom were martyred for their Christian faith.

The Russian Orthodox Church now says that 200,000 priests, monks, and nuns were executed in the 1920s and 1930s, when 45,000 churches were closed or destroyed. I spent time in Yakutsk, in eastern Siberia, where statues of Lenin and Jerzhinsky, the founder of the KGB, still stand. Bishop German of Yakustk told me of the sufferings of the people in this frozen wasteland, where exiles were forced to dig out minerals, just as Christians in the Roman empire were condemned to work in the mines. He told me that when the snow briefly melted in the springtime, they would find the bodies of prisoners who had tried to escape during the winter, when the temperature drops to minus 40 degrees. They called them "snowdrops." Amongst the many Christians martyred were nearly all the priests of his diocese. In 1922 one of the priests of the Trinity Church was thrown into the River Lena to drown. Its surface was frozen solid: they pick-axed the ice to throw him to a freezing death. The Catholic Church saw hundreds of thousands of its members deported to Siberia, Kazakhstan, and remote parts, where they suffered martyrdom. I have stood at the graves of martyrs in Eastern Europe, but the names of many thousands will never be known. Very often the witness and prayers of these "nameless unknown soldiers" (as Pope John Paul II called them) have led to new life in the Church and a surge in vocations to the priesthood and religious life—as has happened in Poland and western Ukraine.

Are Christians being martyred for their faith today?

Some estimate that today, between 250 and 300 million Christians are suffering for their faith or oppressed for their beliefs. From Sudan and Saudi Arabia to Congo and China there are real examples of persecution. I went to China a few years ago and was able to meet Catholic "underground" bishops and priests who had been imprisoned. It is reckoned that at least twenty bishops are in prison, labor camps, or under house arrest for their loyalty to Rome. I met one priest in Inner Mongolia who had spent twelve years in prison. He took me to a Christian cemetery, which the villagers can only visit with the permission of the authorities. There he showed me a clearing where twelve Christians martyred in 1968 had been buried. Four of them were priests, and four of them were sisters who had been stabbed to death. But now over 500 people go to the small village church nearby.

chapter 9

Mystics and Visionaries

Saintly Visions

Many saints are known to have had mystical experiences. Their detachment from this world is rewarded by a privilege that is usually reserved for the next: the immediate and real sensation of the presence of God. The saints who tend to be defined as mystics or visionaries are those whose experiences are so dramatic that they are obvious to witnesses, or who describe them by writing them down. St. John, author of *The Book of Revelation,* teaches with the authority of one who has seen the living God face to face: "His head and his hairs were white like wool, as white as snow; and his eyes were as a flame of fire." (Revelation, 1:14).

St. Augustine (354–430) describes in his *Confessions* a mystical revelation of the meaning of eternity that he experienced jointly with his mother, St. Monica (332–87). Dame Julian of Norwich (1342–c.1416) writes in her *Revelations of Divine Love* of how God "showed me a little thing, the quantity of a hazelnut, lying in the palm of my hand, as it seemed. And it was as round as any ball. I looked upon it with the eye of my understanding, and thought, 'What may this be?' And it was answered generally thus, 'It is all that is made.'"

previous page: **The Vision of St. Augustine, Filippo Lippi, c. 1406–69, Italian**
The saint tells a child trying to empty the sea with a spoon that it is pointless; the child replies that trying to comprehend the immensity of God is equally vain.
right: **St. John the Evangelist, Berto di Giovanni, fl. 1482, Italian**
Revelation is traditionally ascribed to the Apostle and Evangelist.

Marks of Holiness

The most dramatic manifestation of a mystic's closeness to God is the stigmata, in which Christ's wounds are reproduced in the mystic's body. The phenomenon is not known before the thirteenth century; its first appearance coincides with the emergence of devotional writings that encouraged meditation on the sufferings of Jesus.

Some stigmatics only experience the pain endured by Christ during his passion, but others display his physical wounds, too. These can include nail holes in the hands and feet, a spear wound in the side, the marks of scourging on the back, abrasions caused by carrying the cross on the shoulder, and injuries to the head caused by a crown of thorns. More than 300 individuals have been recognized as stigmatics but only sixty-two have been beatified or canonized, for the presence of the stigmata is not considered proof of sainthood.

The first stigmatic was St. Francis of Assisi (1181–1226), who received the stigmata in a dramatic moment on Mount La Verna in 1224. The moment was recorded by the great poet Dante:

**On the harsh crag between
   Tiber and Arno
From Christ did he receive that
   final seal
Which his limbs carried for two years**

DANTE, *PARADISO*, IX

According to *The Little Flowers of St. Francis,* the mountainside was enveloped in a radiant light, as Christ appeared to Francis in the form of a seraph and gave him the unmistakable insignia of his passion—the stigmata:

… his hands and feet appeared to be pierced through the middle with nails, the heads of which were in the palms of his hands and the soles of his feet; and the points came out again in the back of the hands and the feet, and were turned back and clinched in such manner that within the bend formed by the reversal of the points a finger could easily be placed as in a ring; and the heads of the nails were round and black.

THE LITTLE FLOWERS OF SAINT FRANCIS OF ASSISI

Other stigmatic saints followed: St. Rita of Cascia (1377–1447) was an Augustinian nun whose mystical meditations were accompanied by the appearance of the wounds of Christ's crown of thorns on her forehead. They lasted 15 years. Between 1542 and 1554, the Dominican nun St. Catherine Dei Ricci (1522–90) experienced extended ecstasies in which she acted out Christ's passion, with the marks of his sufferings appearing on her body. St. Gemma Galgani (1878–1903) was a laywoman whose desire to become a nun was frustrated by ill health. Intensely prayerful, she experienced the stigmata frequently between 1899 and 1901. She was canonized by Pius XII in 1940.

St. Francis in Art

The story of St. Francis of Assisi has inspired countless works of art. The first biography of the saint who GK Chesterton called "the most unworldy man that ever walked the world" was written by one of Francis' companions, Thomas of Celano (1200–1255). He described the saint in extraordinary, vivid detail:

... a man who spoke freely, of joyous aspect with a benevolent countenance far removed from softness or haughtiness; of average height, indeed rather short; a rotund, not very large head; elongated, thin body; forehead smooth, not broad; medium-size black eyes; ingenuous look; dark hair; straight eyebrows; nose, thin and regular; ears prominent but small; smooth temples; tongue without venom; a voice full of fervor and passion, penetrating, gentle, clear, sorrowful; even, white, strong teeth; small, thin lips; black, unkempt beard; slender neck; straight shoulders; fine hands with long fingers tapering into well-modeled nails; spindly legs; small feet; delicate skin; a minimum of flesh. He dressed in a tunic of coarse fabric; he hardly ever slept and his hand was ever open in an act of generosity. Since he was a humble man among humble men, he demonstrated an infinite mildness toward all, and knew how to adjust to all humors and dispositions. He was the most saintly among saints who, when among sinners, looked like one of them.

THOMAS OF CELANO, *THE LIVES OF ST FRANCIS*

Francis is considered to be one of the most universally popular of all the saints, and his life has been extensively recorded in history, biography, poetry, music, painting and film.

In addition to Thomas of Celano's account of the saint's life, another well-regarded early source is the biography of St Francis written by St. Bonaventure (c. 1218–74). This describes how the author himself had been miraculously cured as a child by the intercession of the saint. *The Little Flowers of St. Francis,* a collection of anecdotes assembled a century after the saint's death, is still in print.

At least a dozen movies have been made about him. The first, *San Francesco il Poverello di Assisi,* appeared in 1911; the most famous, *Brother Sun Sister Moon,* was made by Franco Zeffirelli in 1972. The French mystic composer Olivier Messiaen wrote the libretto as well as the music for his opera *Saint François d'Assise,* which was first performed in 1983.

Some of the finest late medieval and renaissance paintings depict the saint and the key events of his life. A pictorial biography by Benozzo Gozzoli (1420–97) decorates the church of Montefalco, and scenes painted by Cimabue (1240–1302), Giotto (1267–1337) and others adorn the walls of the basilica at Assisi. St. Francis' own inspirational poem in praise of the Creator for his creation, *The Canticle of Brother Sun*, is a simple and direct work of great beauty.

The Canticle of Brother Sun

Praised be my Lord God, with all his creatures: and especially
    our brother the sun, who brings us the day and who brings
    us the light.

Fair is he, and shining with a very great splendor: O Lord, he
    signifies to us thee.

Praised be my Lord for our sister the moon, and for the stars,
    the which he has set clear and lovely in heaven.

Praised be my Lord for our brother the wind, and for air and
    cloud, calms and all weather by the which thou upholdest
    life in all creatures.

Praised be my Lord for our sister water, who is very
    serviceable unto us and humble and precious and clean.

ST. FRANCIS OF ASSISI, *THE CANTICLE OF BROTHER SUN*

left: **St. Francis Preaching to the Birds, Giotto, 1297–1300, Italian**
In this delightful incident, recorded in *The Little Flowers of St. Francis*, the
saint preaches to a flock of birds, reminding them to be grateful to their
Creator. They departed only after he had given them his blessing.

St. Catherine of Siena

The stigmata of St. Catherine of Siena (1347–80) occurred in a mystical experience in 1375, but the marks did not appear outwardly in her body during her life. Five years earlier, she had had a series of mystical experiences in which she had a vision of Purgatory, Heaven, and Hell, and heard a Divine command to enter public life. This gave her the confidence to offer advice to those in authority over the church. When the Great Schism occurred after the death of Pope Gregory XI in 1378, she wrote to cardinals, kings, and princes to urge them to support Pope Urban VI.

Catherine's mysticism began in the innocence of childhood and continued throughout a life of dramatic asceticism; her self-denial expressed her determination to get closer to God. Some have recognized in her extreme fasting a kind of "holy anorexia," but to whatever extent this might be true, it does not make her any less of a saint. Pope Paul VI declared her a Doctor of the Church in 1970 on account of her mystical writings, which include her *Dialogue* and her many letters.

left: **The Ecstasy of St. Catherine of Siena, Agostino Carracci, 1557–1602, Italian**
St. Catherine's stigmata were invisible to others during her life.

Padre Pio

The most recently canonized stigmatic is St. Pius of Pietrelcina (1887–1968), better known as Padre Pio. Franciso Forgione was born in poverty in a village near Naples. He was an intensely religious child, and later in life spoke of his early mystical experiences, in which he would converse with Jesus, Mary, and his guardian angel. He privately consecrated himself to God when he was five. Francesco took the name "Pio" when he became a Capuchin friar in 1903. He was ordained priest in 1910. In 1918, he had two ecstatic visions; in the second of them, he received the stigmata. He described the experience later in a letter:

I saw before me a mysterious person … His hands, feet and side were dripping blood. The sight of him frightened me: what I felt at that moment is indescribable … I became aware that my hands, feet and side were pierced and were dripping with blood.

He covered his wounds and tried to keep them secret, but news got out and huge crowds began to come to the friary to attend his mass, receive his blessing, and go to him for confession. His popularity did not endear him to some in ecclesiastical authority, who seem to have taken Padre Pio's obvious holiness as an affront. Attempts were made to discredit Padre Pio in the eyes of the Vatican, painting him as a fraudster who took sexual advantage of his penitents.

In 1922 Padre Pio's contact with the public was limited; he was forbidden to show or talk about his stigmata or to bless crowds from his window. After popular protests, these restrictions were lifted, but the stream of calumnies continued, and in 1931 the Holy See ordered Padre Pio to cease all priestly activity except the celebration of mass, which was to be in private.

In the face of this injustice, Padre Pio remained silent. In 1933, Pope Pius XI lifted the ban, and his successor, Pope Pius XII, cooperated with him in setting up a "House for the Relief of Suffering"—a hospital, hospice, and retreat center—that was opened in 1956. The success of the project seems to have inspired further resentment and jealousy, and further false accusations of impropriety were made to the Vatican.

Meanwhile, the spirituality of Padre Pio inspired prayer groups that grew and proliferated all over the world. Over a hundred thousand people attended his funeral. An official investigation found that all the accusations that had been made against him were false. He was canonized on June 16th, 2002.

The life and mission of Padre Pio prove that difficulties and sorrows, if accepted out of love, are transformed into a privileged way of holiness …

POPE JOHN PAUL II

St. Hildegard of Bingen

Some scientists explain the wounds of stigmatics by describing them as the physical result of a psychological condition, but nobody has yet produced a scientific explanation of quite how such a cause might bring about such an effect. There are, however, cases in which recognized medical conditions might have contributed to the mystical experiences of the saints. To acknowledge this is not to invalidate their insights, but to account for the context in which they arose. The abbess St. Hildegard of Bingen (1098–1179) likened her ecstasies to visions of "multitudes of sparks" accompanied by "lights more brilliant than the sun." Her description corresponds to the symptoms of migraine, from which she almost certainly suffered.

Hildegard's mysticism was also expressed in art and music. She recorded her visions in a work called *Scivias*, which she completed with the encouragement of St. Bernard and the approval of Pope Eugenius III. She illustrated it herself, with pictures that recall the engravings of the eighteenth-century poet and visionary William Blake. She was also a poet, who wrote hymns, and one of the earliest morality plays, *Ordo Virtutum,* in which the Devil competes for the soul of a woman against seventeen personified virtues. Her other writings include works on natural history and herbal medicine, which although secular in content, celebrate the glory of God's creation. Her exultant yet reflective music expresses a visionary's response to life: she described composing it as "writing, seeing, hearing, and knowing all in one manner."

right: **Hildegard of Bingen, unnamed and undated engraving**
Hildegard's ethereal music has been rediscovered by modern audiences.

St. Teresa of Avila

St. Teresa of Avila (1515–82), like St. Catherine of Siena, was highly religious as a child. One of the most renowned Spanish mystics and monastic reformers, she was born north-west of Madrid at Avila in Old Castile and died at Alba de Tormes (in the province of Salamanca). Teresa grew up with great ascetic ideals. The example of heroic saints and martyrs was instilled in her from her earliest days by her father, Alonso Sánchez de Cepeda, but even more intensely by her mother, Beatriz d'Avila y Ahumada. Her parents' family are thought to have been Jewish converts from Toledo.

Teresa was fascinated by accounts of the lives of the saints: she and her brother once tried to run away to Morocco, where they imagined they would be martyred for their faith. She entered a Carmelite convent at the age of twenty, where she began to cultivate the habit of mental prayer that was later to flower in ecstatic mysticism. She thought the regime at her convent was too relaxed, so she founded a reformed branch of "Discalced" (shoeless) Carmelites, whose members embraced poverty wholeheartedly, wore simple habits of coarse cloth, and followed a simple diet. This strictness was healthily moderated by a sense of balance, in which, as she once said, "there is a time for partridge and a time for penance." She also memorably commented: "May God protect me from gloomy saints!"

right: **St. Teresa of Avila, unattributed portrait, early 17th century, Spanish**
St. Teresa's writings reveal not only her mysticism, but also an attractive and lively human character.

St. Teresa is one of the saints who provide an insight into mysticism through their writings. In *The Interior Castle*, she describes how she "began to think of the soul as if it were a castle made of a single diamond or of very clear crystal, in which there are many rooms, just as in Heaven there are many mansions." For Teresa, "the door of entry into this castle is prayer and meditation: I do not say mental prayer rather than vocal, for, if it is prayer at all, it must be accompanied by meditation." Teresa's prayer led to mystical experiences that she recorded in an autobiography that she wrote at the command of her spiritual director. Its tone is simple and unsentimental, but the visions and ecstasies described are intense, and the wisdom is uplifting.

"The Lord of the Castle … dearly loves humility: if you think yourselves unworthy to enter the third mansion, He will grant you all the sooner the favor of entering the fifth. Then if you serve Him well there, and often repair to it, He will draw you into the mansion where He dwells Himself, where you need never depart … When once you have learned how to enjoy this Castle, you will always find rest, however painful your trials may be, in the hope of returning to your Lord, which no one can prevent." St. Teresa was canonized in 1622 and was awarded the title "Doctor (Teacher) of the Church," in 1970.

St. Teresa's friend and fellow-mystic St. John of the Cross (1542–91) wrote some of Spain's finest lyric poetry and the spiritual classic, *The Dark Night of the Soul.* Teresa encouraged John to join her newly reformed order, which he vigorously defended against the criticisms of the unreformed Carmelites. As a result, he was falsely denounced to the Inquisition, and imprisoned. He escaped after nine months, but was hounded by jealous and resentful opponents for the rest of his life.

Thou art Love's victim, and must die
A death more mystical and high;
Into Love's arms thou shalt let fall
A still-surviving funeral.

RICHARD CRASHAW, *A HYMN TO THE NAME AND HONOR OF THE ADMIRABLE ST. TERESA*

St. Joseph of Copertino

St. Joseph of Copertino (1603–63) had his first ecstatic vision at eight years old, and it is said that when his companions saw him standing as if in a trance, they gave him his nickname, *Bocca Aperta,* "Open-Mouth." However, he might equally have earned the title by gaping when asked questions in school, for he was a remarkably ungifted student. He was accepted as a lay brother by the Capuchins at Martino near Tarento, where his repeated ecstasies were not favorably appreciated, and he was dismissed as a dreamer unfit for work. He then became a stable lad at the Franciscan convent of La Grotella, where his piety was recognized.

Despite his limited intellectual abilities, he was eventually accepted as a candidate for the priesthood, and ordained in 1625. He experienced ecstasies and visions from which others were unable to arouse him—whether by shaking him, sticking him with pins, or burning him with candles. He levitated so frequently that he earned a new nickname, "The Flying Friar." His fellow-friars were unsettled by these supernatural events and by the crowds that gathered to witness them; they didn't know how to handle him. After being interrogated by the Inquisition, he was forbidden to appear in public and was kept out of sight for the next thirty-five years by being moved from convent to convent. He accepted his virtual imprisonment without complaint. He was canonized in 1767 by Clement XIII.

left: **St. Joseph of Copertino, engraving after the painting by Domenico Pecchio, 1686–1760, Italian**

St. Joseph's community recorded seventy instances of his levitation.

St. Bernadette

The ecstasies of St. Bernadette Soubirous (1844–79) took the form of eighteen visions of the Virgin Mary, which the fourteen-year-old girl experienced between February and April 1858. Sent by her mother to gather firewood, she saw a figure in a cave. At first, she did not know who it was.

I saw a girl in white, no bigger than myself, who greeted me with a slight bow of the head … I saw the girl smiling at me most graciously and seeming to invite me to come nearer.

The sixteenth time the lady appeared to Bernadette, she identified herself by saying "I am the Immaculate Conception." Bernadette did not know that this title had been formally promulgated by the pope some four years earlier.

Plagued by publicity and the intrusive enquiries of the curious, Bernadette joined the Sisters of Notre-Dame de Nevers in 1866 and played no part in the development of Lourdes as a center of pilgrimage. She was canonized in 1933—not on account of her visions, but for the absolute virtues that she displayed throughout the whole of her life.

left: **St. Bernadette, unnamed photographer**
The Lourdes visionary was born into extreme poverty.

St. Thérèse of Lisieux

Sanctity and intense spirituality are not always accompanied by spectacular external manifestations. Nobody would have heard of St. Thérèse of Lisieux (1873–1927) if she hadn't been ordered by her superiors to write her spiritual autobiography, *The Story of A Soul*. One writer has called her a "Mystic of the Ordinary." The external events of her life were entirely unremarkable: she was a simple nun in a provincial French convent.

What made her special, though, was the childlike simplicity of her love of God, which made her holiness an inspiration to the few people who met her in life and to the many who know her through her book, which has been translated into more than fifty languages. She taught—and her life showed—that sanctity does not have to be dramatic; it can be reached by following what she called "the little way," in which even the most humdrum tasks are carried out selflessly for the love of God.

She wrote that "God sometimes communicates himself to us in a blinding light, at other times, gently, veiled in symbols and imagery." The image that dominates Thérèse's writings is the flower, and she is popularly known as "The Little Flower of Jesus." She was canonized by Pope Pius XI in 1925 and declared a Doctor of the Church by Pope John Paul II in 1997.

right: **St. Thérèse of Lisieux, embroidered devotional card, Spanish**
St. Thérèse is often shown carrying a bunch of roses that signify the miracles and favors she bestows.

Just as the air on a sunny day seems transformed into sunshine instead of being lit up, so it is necessary for the saints that all human feelings melt in a mysterious way and flow into the will of God.

ST. BERNARD OF CLAIRVAUX

Those who love God, open themselves entirely to him. They ask him to enter their senses, their souls and their minds.

ST. HILDEGARD OF BINGEN

In ecstatic prayer, the Lord catches the soul, just as the clouds gather up the morning mists on earth; and the Lord carries the soul right out of itself, just as the clouds – so I am told – carry the mist towards the sun.

ST. TERESA OF AVILA

God cures our imperfections by putting the soul into a dark night. Through pure dryness and interior darkness he weans us away from the breast of earthly gratifications and delight, and draws us away from all trivial and childish concerns; and he leads us into the path of virtue. Even if we practice every kind of self-mortification with great passion and zeal, we achieve nothing until God purges us by means of the dark night and we passively submit.

ST. JOHN OF THE CROSS

My ordinary way of praying is this: hardly do I begin to pray than at once I feel my soul begin to recollect itself in a peace and tranquillity that I cannot express in words. The senses seem suspended.

PADRE PIO

The word of God has come to me many times, penetrating my soul. Yet I have never been aware of the moment of his coming. I perceive his presence, and I remember afterwards that he has been with me. Sometimes, I even have an inkling that he will come. But I am never conscious of his coming and going, and where he comes from, where he goes after leaving. And by what means he enters and withdraws, I cannot say.

ST. BERNARD OF CLAIRVAUX

For me, prayer is like a ship being launched into the sea; in prayer, I am carried toward God

ST. THÉRÈSE OF LISIEUX

In the highest stage of prayer the soul is conscious that it is fading away in a kind of swoon; it feels very calm, and full of joy. The breath and bodily powers progressively fail, so that you cannot move even the hands without great effort. The eyes close involuntarily; and, if they remain open, they see almost nothing.

ST. TERESA OF AVILA

Our soul is created to be God's home, and the soul is at home in the uncreated God.

DAME JULIAN OF NORWICH

Father, I abandon myself into your hands; do with me what you will. Whatever you may do, I thank you. I am ready for all, I accept all. Let only your will be done in me, and in all your creatures. I wish no more than this, O Lord.

BLESSED CHARLES DE FOUCAULD

Interview with Christopher Howse

Author and Journalist

One of your recent books is an anthology of spiritual writings.
Do any of the writings of the saints reveal much of their human
personalities?

The man who would have made a tremendous novelist is St. Augustine. In his autobiographical Confessions he spends a famous chapter analyzing his state of mind and motives as a boy when he stole some pears from an orchard. He didn't even want the pears, he realizes. You don't get that kind of psychological interest in other writers of his time. Later in his life we get his very words, his tone of voice, and his asides, since trained shorthand writers wrote down his sermons as they were delivered. We get the heat of the church in the port city of Hippo, and the smoke. He admits to the audience that he is getting hoarse, or he notices that they are getting drowsy.

There is a surprising trio of women who have left us with very endearing human life stories, full of detail and personal foibles—the three Teresas—St. Teresa of Avila, St. Thérèse of Lisieux, and St. Edith Stein, whose religious name was Teresa Benedicta of the Cross. They all come across as very real people, with hopes and fears like the rest of us.

Teresa of Avila had a great sense of humor. We catch her laughing at herself, as when she admits to being terribly annoyed by a nun who sits behind her in church and grinds her thumbnail on her teeth. She was extraordinary for a woman in the male-dominated world of imperial Spain. But from her autobiography you can see how disarming she must have been. That's part of how she got so much done. For a nun who insisted on living in an enclosed world she did a great deal of hard traveling. There's a marvelous bit in her Life where she describes a dangerous journey through floods to one of her convents near Burgos. The whole landscape is under water, the carriage keeps getting bogged down in the mud, and at one point, they have to cross a river on pontoons that they can't see for the flooding—"one slip, and they all would be lost," she writes. She admits that she is frightened, even though she completely trusts in God; what is also clear to the reader is her sense of excitement. She is so clear and vivid as a writer. Her prose style is never inflated, and her achievements are all the more remarkable for having been written in snatches, on window ledges between her other duties.

St. Thérèse of Lisieux also reveals herself as a very human person in her writings. I used to think she was a neurotic, but deep down she was amazingly controlled. It's as if she is watching herself feeling anxious but deeper down knowing that there is more to herself than that. Her fellow-nuns thought her always happy, but in her autobiography, she writes of the real suffering that was often behind her smile. Though she espoused the "Little Way" of offering small things to God, she was by no means a wimp. She faced up to illness, tuberculosis and worse, with great toughness. And inside, she felt something bleaker than a dark night. Toward the end of her life, when she was hanging on by faith alone, she wrote: "When I want to restore my heart, exhausted by the darkness that surrounds it, with the memory of the bright country that I aspire to, my torment redoubles. It seems to me that the darkness borrows the voice of sinners and says mockingly to me: "You are dreaming about the light, about a homeland redolent with sweet perfumes. You are dreaming about the eternal possession of the Creator of all these wonders. You believe that one day you will walk out of this fog that surrounds you! Come on. Come on— rejoice in death which will give you not what you hope for, but a night still more profound, the night of nothingness." It is a terrifying predicament for someone who has given her life to God and is on the verge of death. Yet not only does she hold on, but she has the honesty to write down these tormenting thoughts, when ordinary people might prefer to keep them hidden.

Edith Stein writes in her letters about her family, her loves, and her academic plans. She was Jewish, middle class, and by training a philosopher; then she decided to change her life in a way she knew was going to upset people. Not only was she to become a Christian, but she was going to be a Carmelite nun. Many Carmelite nuns are clever, but their way of life is contemplative, not academic. They give up professional life in the world and make prayer their profession.

It seemed like a denial of her vocation as a scholar, and a denial of her birthright as a Jew. But she explains in her later writing how God gives her back more than she loses. As she was being taken by the Nazis, knowing that they would murder her, she said, "I am going for my people." Of course she meant the Jews. But she sees the Cross as entering history here. She would die with Jesus, a Jew like her, in a place that evil men had tried to rid of God. It's very moving. All the uncertainties of her early life, that she had explored so openly in her writings, were resolved by something greater than herself. In the end, she possesses the dignity that her murderers lack.

The limitless loving devotion to God, and the gift God makes of Himself to you, are the highest elevation of which the heart is capable; it is the highest degree of prayer.

ST. EDITH STEIN

chapter 10
Signs and Wonders

Miraculous Events

St Peter's miraculous escape from prison is one of the most dramatic moments in the *Acts of the Apostles:*

"Peter therefore was kept in prison: but prayer was made without ceasing of the church unto God for him. And when Herod would have brought him forth, the same night Peter was sleeping between two soldiers, bound with two chains: and the keepers before the door kept the prison. And, behold, the angel of the Lord came upon him, and a light shined in the prison: and he smote Peter on the side, and raised him up, saying, Arise up quickly. And his chains fell off from his hands. And the angel said unto him, Gird thyself, and bind on thy sandals. And so he did. And he saith unto him, Cast thy garment about thee, and follow me. And he went out, and followed him; and wist not that it was true which was done by the angel; but thought he saw a vision. When they were past the first and the second ward, they came unto the iron gate that leadeth unto the city; which opened to them of his own accord: and they went out, and passed on through one street; and forthwith the angel departed from him."
Acts 12: 5–10

previous page: **Christ Walking on Water, Cristoforo de Predis, c 1440–86, Italian**
"Jesus went unto them, walking on the sea." (Matthew 14: 25)
right: **Liberation of St. Peter, Giovanni Battista Tiepolo, 1696–1770, Italian**
The painting strikingly conveys St. Peter's astonishment.

Saintly Miracles

Saints can be channels of God's miraculous power, or favored beneficiaries of it; they can petition him to exercise it for some special purpose. In each case, the power is not theirs, it is God's, for only God can transcend the laws of nature to effect a miracle. In everyday speech, however, we refer to saints as "performing" the miracles that occur "by their hands" or through their intercession. We acknowledge that such miracles are brought about through their saintliness.

Crediting saints with bringing about miracles is part of the formal process of canonization: a prayer to a holy person that is answered by a miracle is a sign that he or she is a saint. These are almost always instantaneous medical cures that cannot be explained scientifically. The Congregation for the Causes of Saints in the Vatican uses a panel of medical experts to judge on them.

previous page: **St. John the Evangelist Resuscitating Drusiana, Filippino Lippi, 1457–1504, Italian**
A depiction of the version in *The Golden Legend* of a story from the Apocryphal Acts of John.

left: **St. Peter Heals the Sick with his Shadow, Masaccio, 1426–7, Italian**
"… they brought forth the sick into the streets, and laid them on beds and couches, that at the least the shadow of Peter passing by might overshadow some of them." (Acts 5: 15)

next page: **The Marriage Feast at Cana, 16th-century Italian, Venetian School**
The first of Jesus' many miracles was performed at the direct request of his mother, the greatest of the saints (John 2: 1–11).

Then Philip went down to the city of Samaria, and preached Christ unto them. And the people with one accord gave heed unto those things which Philip spake, hearing and seeing the miracles which he did. For unclean spirits, crying with loud voice, came out of many that were possessed with them: and many taken with palsies, and that were lame, were healed. And there was great joy in that city.

ACTS 8: 5-8

And God hath set some in the church, first apostles, secondarily prophets, thirdly teachers, after that miracles, then gifts of healings, helps, governments, diversities of tongues. Are all apostles? are all prophets? are all teachers? are all workers of miracles?

1 CORINTHIANS 12: 28-29

And a certain man lame from his mother's womb was carried, whom they laid daily at the gate of the temple which is called Beautiful, to ask alms of them that entered into the temple ... Then Peter said, Silver and gold have I none; but such as I have give I thee: In the name of Jesus Christ of Nazareth rise up and walk. And he took him by the right hand, and lifted him up: and immediately his feet and ankle bones received strength. And he leaping up stood, and walked, and entered with them into the temple, walking, and leaping, and praising God.

ACTS 3: 2, 6-8

Then all the multitude kept silence, and gave audience to Barnabas and Paul, declaring what miracles and wonders God had wrought among the Gentiles by them.

ACTS 15:12

Then Simon himself believed also: and when he was baptized, he continued with Philip, and wondered, beholding the miracles and signs which were done.

ACTS 8: 13

Padre Pio

The miracle that secured the canonization of St. Pius of Pietrelcina (Padre Pio) occurred in June 2000. Seven-year-old Matteo Pio Colella was admitted to the intensive-care unit of the San Giovanni Rotondo hospital, suffering from meningitis. By the following morning, doctors had lost all hope for him, as so many of his internal organs had failed. Matteo's desperate mother got permission to pray for him at Padre Pio's tomb, and then she and her brother went from convent to convent to beg for prayers from the nuns. That night, during a prayer vigil attended by his mother and some friars from Padre Pio's monastery, his condition suddenly improved. When he awoke from his coma, Matteo said that he had seen an elderly man with a white beard and a long, brown habit—a description of Padre Pio—who said to him, "Don't worry, you will soon be cured." The cure was sudden, lasting, and medically inexplicable.

On December 20th 2001, it was formally recognized as miraculous. Padre Pio was canonized on 16 June 2002.

Prayer is the best weapon we possess, the key that opens the heart of God.

PADRE PIO

right: **Padre Pio (1887–1968), unnamed photographer**
The saint wore mittens to conceal the wounds of the stigmata.

St. Edith Stein

The miracle that was accepted as evidence of the sanctity of St. Edith Stein (Sister Teresa Benedicta of the Cross) occurred on 24th March 1987. Two-year-old Benedicta McCarthy from Brockton, Massachusetts had accidentally taken a large dose of the drug Tylenol. Her liver was irreparably damaged and without a transplant she was certain to die. The child's family and friends prayed to St. Edith Stein, after whom Benedicta had been named. The head of pediatrics at Massachusetts General Hospital was one of several doctors to give evidence to the Congregation for the Causes of Saints that there could be no medical explanation for Benedicta's instantaneous recovery. It was officially recognized as a miracle in 1997. Edith Stein was canonized in 1998.

Those who join the Carmelite Order are not lost to their near and dear ones, but have been won for them, because it is our vocation to intercede to God for everyone.

ST. EDITH STEIN

left: **Edith Stein as a Carmelite Nun, photographed by Otto Bettmann, 1903–98**
A Jewish–born convert to Christianity, St. Edith Stein was murdered in the Nazi concentration camp of Auschwitz in August 1942.

Our Lady of Lourdes

Another official body considers the large number of miraculous cures claimed at the shrine of Our Lady of Lourdes, which was founded after a series of visions experienced by St. Bernadette Soubirous in 1858. The Virgin Mary told the fourteen-year-old of the world's need for prayer and repentance; she instructed her to drink from a spring, and to build a church. St. Bernadette's story was treated sceptically at first, but she stuck to it through exhaustive interrogations and the church authorities eventually accepted it. Lourdes rapidly became a popular center of pilgrimage and many thousands of pilgrims have claimed miraculous cures. In the last hundred years, 6,500 cases have been reported to the Lourdes medical bureau, but fewer than seventy cures have been officially recognized as miraculous.

One of the two miracles that secured the beatification of St. Bernadette in 1925 was the recovery of seventeen-year-old Henri Boisselet from tubercular peritonitis; his condition had been so grave that he received the Last Sacraments. On the last day of a novena (a nine-day prayer cycle) to Bernadette in 1913, he was instantly and totally cured. Passed as fit for military service, he fought in the First World War, was captured, spent nearly three years as a prisoner, and returned home in good health.

right: Mrs. Anthony Geraci Demonstrating her Miracle, photographed by Otto Bettmann, 1903–98
A delighted Mrs. Anthony Geraci at the shrine of Our Lady of Lourdes at St. Lucy's Church, New York in 1939. After immersing her paralyzed foot in the pool, she reported it cured.

Miraculous Improvements

St. Augustine (354–430) recounts numerous miracles that occurred in his North-African community in *The City of God*. Many of them were brought about by the relics of St. Stephen; some of them he witnessed himself. He tells the story of a Syrian called Bassus, who went to pray at St. Stephen's relics for his daughter, who was dangerously ill. He took her dress with him to the shrine. When he got back home, he found that she had died; he threw the dress over her, and she was restored to life.

The miracle which was wrought at Milan when I was there, and by which a blind man was restored to sight, could come to the knowledge of many; for not only is the city a large one, but also the emperor was there at the time, and the occurrence was witnessed by an immense concourse of people ...

ST AUGUSTINE, *CITY OF GOD*

Augustine was recording the events of his own time, but miracles that are written about after the event can grow with the telling. Aftercomers attributed so many miracles to St. Gregory, bishop of Neocaesarea (c.213–70) that he became known as "St. Gregory the Wonderworker." He is said to have made a huge rock move out of the way so that he could build a church, and to have stopped the River Lycus from flooding by planting his staff beside it. The many healings of the sick attributed to St. Gregory are perhaps easier for the modern mind to believe, and the wonders he worked in winning converts are a matter of record. When he was appointed bishop, there were only seventeen people in Neocaesarea who were Christians; when he died, there were only seventeen people who were not.

In *The Legends of the Saints: An Introduction to Hagiography* (1907), Hippolyte Delehaye cites an example that demonstrates how quickly and widely miraculous inventions can spread: "When St. Bernard came to preach the Crusade in the diocese of Constance, an archer in the bodyguard of the Duke of Zahringen scoffed both at the preaching and the preacher by declaring: 'He can no more work miracles than I can.' When the saint came forward to lay his hands on the sick, the scoffer perceived him and fell senseless to the ground, remaining unconscious for some time." Alexander of Cologne adds: "I was quite close to him when this occurred … We called the Abbot, and the poor man was unable to rise until Bernard came to us, offered up a prayer and helped him to his feet." Not one of the eyewitnesses says a word which would suggest a resurrection from death. And yet, a century later, Herbert, the author of a collection of St. Bernard's miracles, Conrad, author of the *Exordium*, and Caesarius of Heisterbach all affirm that the archer fell dead and that the saint restored him to life.

St. Elizabeth of Hungary

Delehaye also describes how later biographers turned a touching story of St. Elizabeth of Hungary (1207–31) into a miracle. In the original version, she finds a leper whose symptoms were so repellent that his carers had abandoned him; she takes him home and puts him in her own bed. When her husband returns and sees what she has done, he expresses outrage and flings back the covers, but "at that instant God Almighty opened the eyes of his soul, and instead of a leper he saw the figure of Christ crucified stretched upon the bed." Thus told, the story is affecting and edifying, but not miraculous; later writers made it so by turning the husband's insight into a physical reality, in which the leper's body is transformed into a bleeding crucifix with outstretched arms.

A child of four years old was fallen into a pit and drowned, and a man came for to take water and espied the dead child, and he was drawn out, and then they vowed him to St. Elizabeth, and he was anon re-established to his first life and health.

THE GOLDEN LEGEND

left: **St. Elizabeth of Hungary from *Butler's Lives of the Saints*, first published 1756–9**
One of many legendary miracles that reflect St. Elizabeth's charity is that when carrying food to the poor, she was challenged by her husband to show what she was hiding; the bread she concealed suddenly turned into roses.

St. Januarius

St. Januarius (d. c. 305,) bishop of Benevento, near Naples, was martyred under the emperor Diocletian. Few other details of his life are known with certainty. Legend describes him as a miraculous survivor of three attempts to execute him, but it is for a very different miracle that Januarius is remembered today. Since 1389, a phial containing a substance said to be his dried blood has spontaneously liquefied when displayed to the faithful. On the saint's day, September 19th, and on other feasts associated with him, the reliquary containing it is held aloft while the congregation in the cathedral of Naples prays for the miracle to occur. It almost always does: as the reliquary is handled and moved about, the solid matter in the glass tube turns to liquid.

The phenomenon baffled scientists for six centuries, particularly since spectroscopic analyses carried out in 1902 and 1989 suggested that the substance is indeed blood, which cannot go from liquid to solid more than once. But those results have subsequently been challenged, and if the substance is not blood, the phenomenon could have a scientific explanation: a thixotropic gel (such as nondrip paint) is solid when still, and turns liquid when moved about. In 1991, Luigi Garlaschelli, a chemist at the University of Pavia, made a gel that looks and behaves like the substance in the reliquary, using ingredients and technology believed available at the time of the relic's first reported liquefaction.

right: The Martyrdom of St. Januarius, Luca Giordano, 1634–1705, Italian
Almost the only certainty about the saint's martyrdom is that it happened.

St. Nicholas

The miracles that have always been attributed to St. Nicholas, the fourth-century bishop of Myra, made him one of the most widely venerated of saints, but those miracles are now largely regarded as the stuff of legend. Most are first described in an account of his life written 500 years after his death.

The legendary St. Nicholas was characterized as having miraculous gifts right from the start: he is said to have stood up and prayed for two hours when he was given his first bath. As an infant, he refused his mother's breast on Fridays and fast days. As an adult, he restored to life three murdered boys who had been pickled in a brinetub, and he appeared in a vision to the emperor Constantine to tell him to free three men condemned to death on a trumped-up charge.

One of the most famous legends about him is that, as bishop of Myra, when the people of the city were starving because of a crop failure, he persuaded the captains of cargo vessels passing through the port to give up a share of their grain; when they arrived at their final destinations, they found their holds had been miraculously refilled. On a pilgrimage to the Holy Land, St. Nicholas calmed a storm and resurrected a dead sailor; another time, he appeared on the deck of a ship that had run aground and physically helped to relaunch it.

When the Moslems took Myra in the eleventh century, the saint's relics were rescued by a raiding party and taken to Bari, in Italy, where they were visited by pilgrims from all over the world, including Russia, of which nation he is a patron saint. The legend of St. Nicholas had such a hold on the popular imagination that he has survived the secularization of Western society—where he has mutated into Santa Claus, a dispenser of material rather than spiritual gifts.

"O Help us, good Nicolas!
Our ship is full of foam!"
He walked across the waves to them
And led them safely home.

ERIC CROZIER, LIBRETTO FOR BENJAMIN BRITTEN'S CANTATA, *ST. NICOLAS*

next page: **St. Nicholas of Myra, Fra Angelico, 1400–1455, Italian**
St. Nicholas meets the imperial legate; he saves a load of grain for the city of
Myra; he saves a ship, miraculously, from sinking. The range and nature of the
saint's legendary miracles suggest that the historical character that inspired
them was a man driven by powerful generosity and a sense of justice.

A Holy Modern Cure

In 1996 Peter Changu Shitima, a young catechist from Zambia, was diagnosed with terminal AIDS and sent home to die. Changu had a particular devotion to Blessed Luigi Scrosoppi (1804–84), the Italian Oratorian priest who had founded orphanages and homes for the handicapped, and who had gathered together a team of lay helpers that turned itself into an order of nuns. Scrosoppi had been beatified in 1981, but not yet declared a saint.

The miracle needed for his canonization had not yet been recognized. Knowing of Changu's high regard for Blessed Luigi, his parishioners organized prayers to him, and Changu petitioned him, too. On the night of October 9th, 1996, Changu had a dream in which Blessed Luigi appeared to him; the next morning, he woke up feeling perfectly recovered.

One of his doctors, Dr. Pete de Toit, said: "I sent him home because he was a terminal patient, and he returned brimming with health." After the usual investigations, the cure was recognized as miraculous on July 1st 2000, and Blessed Luigi was canonized on June 10th 2001. A healthy Peter Changu was present at the ceremony.

From earth's wide bounds, from
    ocean's farthest coast,
Through gates of pearl streams in
    the countless host,
And singing to Father, Son, and
    Holy Ghost:
Alleluia, Alleluia!

WILLIAM W. HOW, *FOR ALL THE SAINTS*

Mention an historical miracle, and the man unfamiliar with Catholic truth denies it at once: without consideration of the evidence. But when you are discussing with Catholics an historical event in which the marvelous may have entered you get free discussion, one man saying he believes in the miracle and giving his reasons, another saying he does not and giving his reasons ...

HILAIRE BELLOC

The value of miracles comes when we reach the process of proving that the Church is right in representing the Hero of the Gospels as Incarnate God.

RONALD KNOX

The purpose of miracles is to teach us to see the miraculous everywhere.

ST. AUGUSTINE OF HIPPO

And lo, Christ walking on the water, Not of Gennesareth, but Thames!

FRANCES THOMSON, *THE KINGDOM OF GOD*

The believers in miracles accept them (rightly or wrongly) because they have evidence for them. The disbelievers in miracles deny them (rightly or wrongly) because they have a doctrine against them.

GK CHESTERTON

Glossary

Acta: 'Acts' (Latin word)—a biography.

Blessed Sacrament: the bread that when consecrated at the Eucharist becomes the body of Christ.

Catechumens: people who have resolved to become Christians and are undergoing religious education before baptism.

Consecrate: make holy, dedicate; to bless the bread and wine at the Eucharist, thus turning them into the body and blood of Christ.

Eucharist: the central act of Christian worship in which Christ's saving sacrifice is commemorated and continued in a reenactment of the Last Supper.

Hagiography: the study of the lives of the saints.

Partition: dividing up the remains of a saint's body to produce a greater number of relics.

Patriarch: a bishop with authority over a branch of the Orthodox church.

Passio: "Passion" (Latin word)—a record of the sufferings of Christ or a martyr.

Religious relic: a memento of a holy person that is left after his or her death. It can be the body, or what remains of it; it can be something that person wore or used. It can be the instrument of a martyr's torture or death. It can be a part of any of these things.

Rogation days: Days of prayer to appease God's anger at man's sins, to ask protection in calamities, and to obtain a good harvest; in the Middle Ages, they were marked by public processions and ceremonies.

Translation: the transfer of a saint's remains from one tomb or shrine to another.

Biographies of Interviewees

The Rt Rev. Richard Harries DD FKC FRSL has been Bishop of Oxford since 1987. Before that he was Dean of King's College, London, a parish priest and a lecturer in Christian Doctrine and Ethics. He is a frequent contributor to BBC Radio's *Thought for the Day.*

Neville Kyrke-Smith is a former Anglican clergyman, who is now UK Director of Aid to the Church in Need, a Catholic charity founded in 1947 to help Christians persecuted for their faith or in pastoral need. He has traveled extensively throughout Eastern Europe and parts of the Far East.

Father Andrew Louth, MA, MTH, DD is Professor of Patristic and Byzantine Studies at the University of Durham, and author of several books including, most recently, *St. John Damascene: Tradition and Originality in Byzantine Theology* (2002).

Christopher Howse is Letters Editor of The Daily Telegraph and the author of several books on Christian subjects, including *Prayers for this Life* (2005) and *The Best Spiritual Readings Ever* (2002).

Picture credits

Corbis

p. 2 © Jonathan Blair/Corbis; p. 27 © Fine Art Photographic Library/Corbis; p. 47 © Alinari Archives/Corbis; pp 112–113 © Bettmann/Corbis; p. 138 © Bettmann/Corbis; p. 148 © Arte & Immagini srl/Corbis; pp. 166–167 © National Gallery Collection: By kind permission of the Trustees of the National Gallery, London/Corbis; p. 177 © Francis G. Mayer/Corbis; p. 211 © Archivo Iconografico, S.A./Corbis; pp. 232–233 © Arte & Immagini srl/Corbis; p. 237 © Archivo Iconografico, S.A./Corbis; p. 241 © Alinari Archives/Corbis; p. 242 © Burstein Collection/Corbis; pp. 250–251 © Brooklyn Museum of Art/Corbis; pp. 276–277 © Fine Art Photographic Library/Corbis; p. 283 © National Gallery Collection: By kind permission of the Trustees of the National Gallery, London/Corbis; p. 305 © Bettmann/Corbis; pp. 308–309 © Sandro Vannini/Corbis; p. 310 © Alinari Archives/Corbis; p. 313 © Alinari Archives/Corbis; p. 315 © The State Russian Museum/Corbis; p. 317 © Bettmann/Corbis; p. 318 © Francis G. Mayer/Corbis; p. 323 © Hulton-Deutsch Collection/Corbis; pp. 324–325 © Bettmann/Corbis; p. 329 © Bettmann/Corbis; p. 332 © Pizzoli Alberto/Corbis Sygma; p. 342 © Bettmann/Corbis; p. 351 © Arte & Immagini srl/Corbis; p. 356 © Elio Ciol/Corbis; p. 358 © Alinari Archives/Corbis; p. 365 © Archivo Iconografico, S.A./Corbis; pp. 382–383 © Archivo Iconografico, S.A./Corbis; pp. 386–387 © Sandro Vannini/Corbis; p. 396 © Bettmann/Corbis; p. 399 © Bettmann/Corbis; p. 405 © National Gallery Collection: By kind permission of the Trustees of the National Gallery, London/Corbis; pp. 408–409 © Arte & Immagini srl/Corbis;

Mary Evans Picture Library

p. 13; p. 19; pp. 24–25; p. 28; p. 39; p. 40; pp. 42–43; p. 44; p. 55; p. 49; p. 54; p. 82; p. 115; p. 116; p. 119; p. 124; p. 130; pp. 144–145; p. 152; p. 156; p. 173; 182–183; p. 185; p. 189; p. 193; pp. 196–197; p. 204; p. 207; p. 208; pp. 216–217; pp. 220–221; p. 223; pp. 228–229; p. 235; p. 245; p. 253; p. 256; p. 395; p. 261; p. 265; pp. 270—271; p. 273; pp. 284–285; p. 287; p. 292; p. 295; p. 330; pp. 340–341; p. 363; p. 368; p. 370; p. 373; p. 395

SuperStock

p. 4 © Superstock/Civic Museum, Padua, Italy; pp. 10–11 © Superstock/Chapel Sassetti, Saint Trinity, Florence; p. 16 Silvio Fiore/SuperStock/Saint Sebastien Chapel, Lanslevillard, France; p. 31 © Silvio Fiore/SuperStock/Galleria Sabauda, Torino, Italy; pp. 32–33 © SuperStock, Inc. National Gallery Collection: By kind permission of the Trustees of the National Gallery, London; p. 34 © Christie's Images/SuperStock; p. 50 © Stock Montage/SuperStock; p. 52 © SuperStock, Inc./SuperStock; pp. 62–63 © SuperStock, Inc./SuperStock/Alte Pinakothek, Munich, Germany; p. 65 © SuperStock, Inc./SuperStock;

Patron Saints

A

ACCOUNTANTS
St. Matthew

ACTORS
St. Genesius

ADDICTS
St. Maximilian Mary
Kolbe

ADVERTISING
St. Bernardine of Siena

AIDS PATIENTS
St. Peregrine Laziosi

AIR TRAVELERS
St. Joseph of Copertino

ALCOHOLICS
Venerable Matt Talbot,
St. Monica

ALTAR SERVERS
St. John Berchmans

ANESTHETISTS
St. Rene Goupil

ANIMALS
St. Francis of Assisi

ARCHAEOLOGISTS
St. Helen

ARCHITECTS
St. Thomas the Apostle

ARGENTINA
Our Lady of Lujan

ARTISTS
St. Luke, St. Catherine of
Bologna, Blessed Fra
Angelico

ASTRONAUTS
St. Joseph of Copertino

ASTRONOMERS
St. Dominic

ATHLETES
St. Sebastian

ATTORNEYS
St. Thomas More,
St. Raymond of Penyafort

AUSTRALIA
Our Lady Help of
Christians

AUTHORS
St. Francis de Sales

B

BABIES
Feast of the Holy
Innocents

BAKERS
St. Elizabeth of Hungary,
St. Nicholas

BANKERS
St. Matthew

BAPTISM
St. John the Baptist

BARBERS
SS. Cosmas and Damian,
St. Louis of France,
St. Martin de Porres

BEE KEEPERS
St. Ambrose

BEGGARS
St. Alexis, St. Giles

BELGIUM
St. Joseph

BLACKSMITHS
St. Dunstan

BLIND
Raphael, St. Lucy

BODILY ILLS
Our Lady of Lourdes

BOOKKEEPERS
St. Matthew

BOOKSELLERS
St. John of God

BRAZIL
Feast of the Immaculate
Conception

BREAST DISEASE, AGAINST
St. Agatha

BREWERS
St. Luke, St. Augustine of
Hippo, St. Nicholas

BRICKLAYERS
St. Stephen

BRIDES
St. Nicholas

BROADCASTERS
St. Gabriel

BUILDERS
St. Barbara, St. Vincent
Ferrer

BUTCHERS
St. Anthony the Abbot,
St. Luke

C

CAB DRIVERS
St. Fiacre

CANADA
SS. Ann and Joachim,
St. Joseph

CANCER PATIENTS
St. Peregrine Laziosi

CARPENTERS
St. Joseph

CHARITIES
St. Vincent de Paul

CHILDBIRTH
St. Gerard Majella,
St. Raymond Nonnatus

CHILDREN
St. Nicholas

CHILE
Our Lady of Mount
Carmel, St. James the
Greater

CHINA
St. Joseph

CIVIL SERVANTS
St. Thomas More

CLERGY
St. Gabriel of Our Lady of
Sorrows

COLOMBIA
St. Louis Bertrand,
St. Peter Claver

COMMUNICATION WORKERS
St. Gabriel

COMPUTERS
St. Isidore of Seville

CONSTRUCTION WORKERS
St. Thomas the Apostle

COOKS
St. Thomas the Apostle,
St. Lawrence

COURT CLERKS
St. Thomas More

D

DAIRY WORKERS
St. Brigid of Kildare

DANCERS
St. Vitus

DEACONS
St. Stephen

DEAFNESS
St. Francis de Sales

DENMARK
St. Ansgar, St. Canute

DENTISTS
St. Apollonia

DESPERATE CAUSES
St. Jude

DIFFICULT MARRIAGES
St. Rita of Cascia

DISABLED
St. Giles

DISASTERS
St. Genevieve

DOCTORS
St. Luke

DOGS
St. Roch

DOMINICAN REPUBLIC
St. Dominic

DRIVERS
St. Fiacre

DRUG ADDICTION
St. Maximilian Mary
Kolbe

E

EARACHES
St. Polycarp

EARTHQUAKES
St. Francis Borgia

ECOLOGY
St. Francis of Assisi

ECUADOR
Sacred Heart

EDITORS
St. John Bosco

ENGINEERS
St. Patrick,
St. Ferdinand III

ENGLAND
St. Augustine of
Canterbury, St. George,
St. Gregory the Great

EPILEPSY
St. Dymphna, St. Vitus,
St. Willibrord

EUROPE
St. Benedict, St. Bridget,
St. Catherine of Siena

EYE DISORDERS
St. Clare, St. Lucy

F

EALSELY ACCUSED
St. Raymond Nonnatus

FARMERS
St. Isidore the Farmer

FATHERS
St. Joseph

FIREFIGHTERS
St. Florian, St. John of God

FISHERMEN
St. Andrew, St. Peter
(SS. Peter and Paul)

FLORISTS
St. Thérèse of Lisieux, St.
Rose of Lima, St. Dorothy

FRANCE
Our Lady of the
Assumption, St. Denis,
St. Joan of Arc

FUNERAL DIRECTORS
St. Joan of Arc

G

GAMBLING, COMPULSIVE
St. Bernardine of Siena

GARDENERS
St. Adelard, St. Fiacre

GERMANY
St. Boniface, SS. Michael,
Gabriel and Raphael,
St. Peter Canisius,
St.George

GRANDPARENTS
SS. Ann and Joachim

GRAVEDIGGERS
St. Anthony the Abbot

GREECE
St. Andrew, St. Nicholas

GROCERS
SS. Michael, Gabriel and
Raphael

GROOMS
St. Louis of France, St.
Nicholas

H

HAIRDRESSERS
St. Martin de Porres

HAPPY DEATH
St. Joseph

HEADACHES
St. Teresa of Avila

HEART PATIENTS
St. John of God

HOMELESS
St. Benedict, Joseph Labre

HORSES
St. Martin of Tours

HOSPITAL ADMINISTRATORS
St. Frances Xavier Cabrini

HOSPITALS
St. Camillus de Lellis,
St. John of God

HOTEL KEEPERS
St. Amand

HOUSEWIVES
SS. Ann and Joachim,
St. Martha

HUNGARY
St. Gerard, St. Stephen

I

IMPOSSIBLE CAUSES
St. Frances Xavier
Cabrini, St. Rita of Cascia

INDIA
Our Lady of the
Assumption

INFERTILITY
St. Rita of Cascia,
St. Philomena

INSANITY
St. Dymphna

INTERNET
St. Isidore of Seville

INVALIDS
St. Roch

IRELAND
St. Brigid of Kildare,
St. Patrick, St. Columba

ITALY
St. Francis of Assisi,
St. Bernardine of Siena,
St. Catherine of Siena

J

JAPAN
St. Francis Xavier,
St. Peter Baptist and
Companions

JEWELERS
St. Eligius

JORDAN
St. John the Baptist

JOURNALISTS
St. Francis de Sales

JUDGES
St. John of Capistrano

K

KIDNEY DISEASE
St. Benedict

KNEE PROBLEMS
St. Roch

L

LABORERS
St. Isidore the Farmer,
St. James the Greater

LAWYERS
St. Thomas More,
St. Raymond of Penyafort

LEARNING
St. Ambrose

LIBRARIANS
St. Jerome

LITHUANIA
St. Casimir

LONGEVITY
St. Peter

LOST ITEMS
St. Anthony of Padua

LOVERS
St. Valentine

M

MAIDS, DOMESTIC WORKERS
St. Zita of Lucca

MARRIED WOMEN
St. Monica

MEDICAL TECHNICIANS
St. Albert the Great

MENTALLY ILL
St. Dymphna

MERCHANTS
St. Francis of Assisi,
St. Nicholas

MESSENGERS
SS. Michael, Gabriel and
Raphael

METAL WORKERS
St. Eligius

MEXICO
Our Lady of Guadalupe

MIDWIVES
St. Raymond Nonnatus

MISCARRIAGE, PREVENTION
St. Catherine of Sweden

MISSIONARIES
St. Francis Xavier,
St. Thérèse of Lisieux

MONKS
St. John the Baptist

MOTHERS
St. Monica

MUSICIANS
St. Cecilia

N

NETHERLANDS
St. Willibrord

NEUROLOGICAL DISEASES
St. Dymphna

NEW ZEALAND
Our Lady Help of
Christians

NICARAGUA
St. James the Greater

NIGERIA
St. Patrick

NORTH AFRICA
St. Cyprian

NORTH AMERICA
Isaac Jogues, John de
Brébeuf and Companions

NORWAY
St. Olaf

NOTARIES
St. Luke, St. Mark

NUNS
St. Scholastica, St. Brigid
of Kildare

NURSES
St. Camillus de Lellis, St.
John of God, St. Agatha

O

OBSTETRICIANS
St. Raymond Nonnatus

ORATORS
St. John Chrysostom

ORPHANS, ABANDONED
CHILDREN
St. Jerome Emiliani

P

PAINTERS
St. Luke

PARAGUAY
Our Lady of the
Assumption

PARALYSIS
St. Osmund

PARENTHOOD
St. Rita of Cascia

PARISH PRIESTS
St. John Vianney

PAWNBROKERS
St. Nicholas

PENITENTS
St. Mary Magdalene

PERFUMERS
St. Mary Magdalene

PERU
St. Joseph, St. Rose of
Lima

PHARMACISTS
SS. Cosmas and Damian

PHILIPPINES
St. Rose of Lima

PHILOSOPHERS
St. Catherine of
Alexandria, St. Albert the
Great

PHYSICIANS
St. Luke, SS. Cosmas and
Damian

PILOTS
St. Joseph of Copertino,
St. Thérèse of Lisieux

POETS
St. Columba, St. David

POISONING
St. Benedict

POLAND
St. Casimir, St. Florian,
St. Stanislaus

POLICE OFFICERS
SS. Michael, Gabriel and
Raphael

POLITICIANS, PUBLIC
SERVANTS
St. Thomas More

POOR
St. Anthony of Padua,
St. Laurence

POPES
St. Peter (Peter and Paul)

PORTUGAL
St. George

POSTAL WORKERS
SS. Michael, Gabriel and
Raphael

PREACHERS
St. John Chrysostom

PREGNANT WOMEN
SS. Ann and Joachim,
St. Gerard Majella,
St. Margaret

PRIESTS
St. John Vianney

PRINTERS
St. Augustine, St. John
of God

PRISONERS
St. Dismas, St. Joseph
Cafasso

PUBLIC RELATIONS
St. Bernardine of Siena

R

RADIO
SS. Michael, Gabriel and
Raphael

RADIOLOGISTS
SS. Michael, Gabriel and
Raphael

RECONCILIATION
St. Vincent Ferrer

RETREATS
St. Ignatius of Loyola

RHEUMATISM
St. James the Greater

ROME
St. Peter and St. Paul

RUSSIA
St. Andrew, St. Basil the
Great, St. Casimir,
St. Nicholas, St. Joseph

S

SAILORS
St. Elmo, St. Brendan, St.
Francis of Paola

SCHOLARS
St. Brigid of Kildare, St.
Bede the Venerable

SCHOOLCHILDREN
St. Benedict

SCHOOLS
St. Thomas Aquinas

SCIENTISTS
St. Albert the Great

SCOTLAND
St. Margaret, St. Andrew

SCULPTORS
St. Claude

SECRETARIES
St. Genesius

SEMINARIANS
St. Charles Borromeo

SERBIA
St. Sava

SERVANTS
St. Sava, St. Zita of Lucca

SHEPHERDS
St. Marie Bernadette
Soubirous, St. Paschal
Baylon

SICK
St. John of God

SKIN DISEASES
St. Anthony the Abbot

SLAVIC PEOPLES
SS. Cyril and Methodius

SOBRIETY
Venerable Matt Talbot

SOCIAL WORKERS
St. Louise de Marillac

SOLDIERS
St. George, St. Martin of Tours

SOUTH AFRICA
Our Lady of the Assumption

SOUTH AMERICA
St. Rose of Lima

SPAIN
St. James the Greater

SPEAKERS
St. John Chrysostom

STOMACH DISORDERS
SS. Timothy and Titus

STUDENTS
St. Catherine of Alexandria, St. Thomas Aquinas

SURGEONS
SS. Cosmas and Damian, St. Luke

SWEDEN
St. Bridget of Sweden

SWITZERLAND
St. Nicholas von Flue

T

TAILORS
St. Homobonus

TAX COLLECTORS
St. Matthew

TAXI DRIVERS
St. Fiacre

TEACHERS
St. Gregory the Great, St. John Baptist de la Salle

TEENAGERS
St. Aloysius Gonzaga, St. Maria Goretti

TELECOMMUNICATIONS
Gabriel (Michael, Gabriel and Raphael)

TELEVISION
St. Clare

THEATRICAL PERFORMERS
St. Genesius

THEOLOGIANS
St. Alphonsus Liguori, St. Augustine of Hippo

THROAT AILMENTS
St. Blase

TOOTHACHE
St. Apollonia

TRAVELERS
St. Anthony of Padua, St. Nicholas, St. Joseph, SS. Michael, Gabriel and Raphael

TURKEY
St. John the Apostle

U

UNDERTAKERS
SS. Joseph of Arimathea and Nicodemus

UNITED STATES
Feast of the Immaculate Conception

UNIVERSITIES
Blessed Contardo Ferrini

URUGUAY
SS. Philip and James

V

VENEZUELA
Our Lady of Coromoto

VETERINARIANS
St. Eligius

VIETNAM
St. Joseph

VINTNERS
St. Amand

VOCATIONS
St. Alphonsus Liguori

W

WALES
St. David

WEAVERS
St. Anthony Claret

WEST INDIES
St. Gertrude

WIDOWS
St. Frances of Rome, St. Paula

WOMEN IN LABOR
SS. Ann and Joachim, St. Elmo

WORKERS
St. Joseph

WRITERS
St. Francis de Sales

Y

YOUTH
St. Aloysius Gonzaga, St. Maria Goretti, St. John Bosco

Index

Page numbers in *italics* refer to captions/ illustrations
Page numbers in **bold**, indicate main references

First published by MQ Publications Limited

12 The Ivories

6–8 Northampton Street

London, N1 2HY

email: mqpublications.com

website: www.mqpublications.com

ISBN (10)   1-84601-002-0

ISBN (13)   978-1-84601-002-6

10 9 8 7 6 5 4 3 2 1

Printed and bound in China